"*Wild at Heart* is an emoti

narrative power is percept

and wise strategies offer a fresh and pow

cooperation and trust of teenagers. An inspiring must-read for everyone who desires to effectively relate with adolescents!"

~Debbie Pell, M.Ed., a 33-year veteran in the field of special education, serving on local and state boards in advocacy for students with special needs. Director and Co-Owner of The Dominion School, a private, therapeutic day school serving adolescents with severe emotional issues that impede academic potential.

"As a mother, 30-year therapist and lifelong horseman, I celebrate the insights and honest, practical connections made in this book. Awareness is the most important tool we can put to use in our lives, and Heather's book offers plenty. Through her knowledge and shared stories, she invites the adult reader to deepen their understanding of adolescents, horses, and even themselves. You will gain invaluable information with each turn of the page!"

~Melisa Pearce, CEO, Touched by a Horse. Inc., Founder of the EGCMethod and Author of *Eponalisa*

"This lovely book explores the many parallels and the few convergences between teens and horses. Heather has a genuinely kind spirit and wise insight into both. Quick and simple ideas, yet a powerful read!"

~Shannon Knapp, M.A., founder of *Horse Sense of the Carolinas* and author of *More than a Mirror: Horses, Humans, and Therapeutic Practices*

"It's easy to connect with this book on many levels, even for those without equine experiences. The author leaves you with many valuable insights into the mentality and viewpoints of adolescents—insights that are crucial to the development of healthy, loving and respectful relationships between parents and their children. I am impressed by the way Ms. Kirby has unraveled the mysteries of the teen for us mere parents to understand. A very valuable resource to keep close at hand during those teenage years."

~Erin H. Hill, Parent

"Heather has the phenomenal gift of being able to speak "teen" and bridge the communication gap between teenagers and adults. *Wild at Heart* is an impressive guide for every adult to better understand the teenagers in their life with straightforward advice that works! Heather weaves her expertise of teens and horses into a fresh perspective that will open your eyes to the WHYS of teenage behavior. This book will help you ease up on the reins of controlling your teenager and develop a relationship based on trust, patience and understanding. A Win/Win!"

~Devon Combs, CEO of Beyond the Arena, LLC,
Certified Equine Gestalt Coach, Author and lifelong horsewoman

"Heather Kirby has written a very useful and wonderfully readable book on the unique relationship between adults and adolescents. Correlating the similarities and differences between the behaviors and emotions of horses and adolescents, Heather demonstrates how adults can engage with their teens to move these relationships toward genuine transformation and healing. Clinicians will find *Wild at Heart* helpful and highly enlightening. Everyone else will find it a joy."

~Peter J Smith, MRE, MDiv, MSW, PhD, Clinical Faculty,
University of Maryland School of Social Work

"Horses offer insights into the minds and hearts of adolescents. Through the use of stories and specific examples, Heather demonstrates the parallels, differences and subtleties that horses reveal about the world of adolescents. This book will inspire all those who are interested in deepening their relationships with adolescents as they help them to heal, learn, and grow."

~Rob Meltzer, M.A.

Wild at Heart

Wild at Heart

Adolescents, Horses & Other Kindred Spirits

Heather H. Kirby, LCSW, CSAC, M.Ed.
&
Certified Equine Gestalt Coach™

MERRY DISSONANCE PRESS CASTLE ROCK, COLORADO

Wild at Heart: Adolescents,
Horses & Other Kindred Spirits

Published by Merry Dissonance Press, LLC
Castle Rock, CO

heather@kcclinicalsolutions.com
www.KCClinicalSolutions.com

Library of Congress Control Number: 2013950211
Kirby, Heather H., Author
Wild at Heart: Adolescents, Horses & Other Kindred Spirits
Heather H. Kirby

ISBN 978-1-939919-61-8
1. Adolescent Psychology
2. Horses

Book Design and Cover Design © 2013
Cover Design by Merry Dissonance Press, LLC
Book Design by Andrea Costantine
Editing by Donna Mazzitelli

Dedication

This book is dedicated to all the horses and teens who have taken the time to teach me how to earn their respect, trust and cooperation.

Contents

Acknowledgments

Life is a journey, not a destination...and none of us travel alone. When we arrive at a significant point in our journey we need to stop and pay tribute to those who have helped pave our road. Writing this book is definitely a milestone in my life, and I want to take this opportunity to publicly acknowledge the many remarkable people, pets, and places that have played a major part in getting me to this point. Listed in order of their appearance in my life, this book is dedicated to...

Priscilla Keith Kirby, my mom, who first inspired my love of horses and who loved me unconditionally through my own turbulent adolescence. For several years, she spent almost an entire day each week driving me back and forth to horseback riding lessons. Every Saturday, she waited patiently while I tacked and rode, then delivered me back home...all with very little appreciation from me until much later in my life. She is truly the person most responsible for my love of horses, which in turn inspired the theories in this book.

William Asa Kirby, my father, who always encouraged me to live with honesty and to pursue my heart's passion, even when it didn't seem practical. In so doing, he has been instrumental in bringing this book to life.

Ellie Kenyon, Dennis McFadden and Denise Perrino, three remarkable teachers from my years at **Oakton High School** in Vienna, VA. While most of my other teachers saw me as a difficult adolescent, these three saw beyond the anger and the attitude to the hidden potential. They each earned my respect and cooperation in ways that later became a framework for my own work with adolescents. In many ways they were the first who helped germinate the ideas in this book and like all good mentors, they have NO idea the profound effect their guidance had on me at an impressionable time in my life.

Debra Schiavone, my own therapist, who for several years in my twenties helped me go back and work through all the residual pain and confusion of my own adolescence. She is almost solely responsible for helping me move into healthy adulthood. For her understanding, patience, and good counsel, I will be forever grateful.

Wediko Children's Services in New Hampshire, where I worked for four influential summers and really began to experience the principles described in this book. Among the amazingly talented staff, special recognition is due to…

> **Joe Langione**, who, in my first summer at Wediko, encouraged me to "make mistakes of commission, not mistakes of omission." I have since applied his advice to not only how I work with teens, but how I live my life.

Tom Hayes, who, in my second summer at Wediko, recognized my capacity for working with teens and urged me to avoid burnout by learning to take care of myself. Without his influence I am certain I would have tired of the difficult work with troubled teens long ago…instead, I continue to love it!

The wonderful staff and trainers at the **National Center for Therapeutic Riding** in Washington, D.C., where many of the ideas in this book were inspired during the year in which I volunteered with them. Their names I have forgotten, but their influence remains strong.

Vinny Froehlich of **Second Genesis** in Alexandria, VA, who took a chance and gave me my first job in the field of substance abuse treatment, even before I was certified. He also taught me the valuable lesson that adolescence is not defined by age but by stage of development. The immense value in this simple lesson of understanding adolescence as a unique stage of development will be evident throughout this book.

George W. Bailey, my mentor and friend from the five years I worked at **Inova Kellar Center** in Fairfax, VA. George's impact on my life cannot be put into words. He was, and remains, the most talented clinician I have ever had the privilege of working with, and he taught me more about effectively working with teenagers than any other single individual in my life. The interest that he took in my career development and the opportunities he provided when I was still early in my career will remain a gift I can never repay. If I could only dedicate this book to one person, it would most certainly be George.

Debbie Pell, my mentor and friend from the six years I worked at **The Dominion School** in Springfield, VA. Debbie believed in my abilities when I was fresh out of graduate school and gave me both guidance and freedom to develop what would become my own style of working with teens. Her servant leadership style and her ability to bring out the best in those who work for and with her are nothing short of remarkable. I unashamedly admit that I aspire "to be like Debbie when I grow up." If I can be half the leader that she is, I will be content.

Roger Rothman, my clinical supervisor while working toward my LCSW. Roger challenged me to think creatively and strategically in my work with adolescents. His tutelage for several years gave me guidance and confidence and helped me further develop the principles presented in this book. Many years later, I still seek his wisdom when I feel stuck.

The many staff, students, and parents of **Accotink Alternative Learning Center** in Springfield, VA, where for five years I applied and refined the practice of looking at teens through the lens described in this book. When I left that program to dedicate myself to completing and publishing this work, my influence on that program was clearly evident. Less evident, but equally significant, is the influence that program has had on me and my professional development.

Melisa Pearce, who I met at an Equine Extravaganza in Richmond, VA in October of 2008. Immediately upon hearing Melisa's presentation, I knew that she would be my next mentor. The founder of **Touched By A Horse**™ in Boulder, Colorado, Melisa combines clinical training with horse expertise and energy awareness to do truly amazing work with clients. She brought me into her certification program, welcomed me into her home, generously shared her insights, and offered me guidance and friendship. She has encouraged the writing of this book in multiple ways. For her generous and open spirit and for the brilliant example she provides, I am indebted.

My fellow students in the **Equine Gestalt Coaching Method™ Certification Program** who have shared with me an incredible journey. Most especially, **Devon Combs, Marie Delmar, Martha Keul, and Terri Mongait**, who were also in the Genesis Group that blazed a trail in Melisa's new program.

Annie Delp, founder and CEO of **Eagle Hill Equine Rescue** in Culpepper, VA. Annie was the first to offer me a concrete opportunity to develop the kind of program for teens and horses that I imagined. While our paths have gone in different directions, her tireless enthusiasm and spirit of generosity remain an inspiration.

The "barn staff," clinical team, and healing herd of horses at the **Alice C. Tyler Village of Childhelp East** in Lignum, VA, where I served for one year as the head of the equine department and had the distinct privilege of creating an equine therapy program for the children in residential treatment. For a time, the job felt like a dream come true.

Darcy Woessner of **Project Horse, Inc.**, who has generously offered me the opportunity to partner with her and her herd of healing horses at a gorgeous facility in Purcelleville, VA. By the time this book goes to print, I imagine she and I will be busy bringing rescue horses together with troubled teens and their families, actively applying and refining the principles in this book.

Donna Mazzitelli, my editor and publisher, who provided extraordinary support in the form of humor, encouragement, patience and good counsel throughout the process of bringing this book to life.

Life's journey is nothing if not shared with special people and animals. The following friends and family members, while not necessarily contributing to the ideas inherent in this book, have contributed to my life in immeasurable ways. Without them, the journey would be drudgery and the book hardly worth writing. Listed in alphabetical order, the following people and animals have given friendship, support, and love over many years, and for their role in my life, I am grateful...**Dawn Calahan, Heidi Carlson, Kelly Cregan, Nancy Graham, Erin Hill, Tanya Hull, KC, Pam Kirby, Licorice, Bob and Peggy MacArthur, Mary Martin, Mason, Sally Patton, Heather Scott, Liz Schnelzer, Up To Somethin' and Linda Kirby Walter.**

Introduction

In a battle of wills, would you rather be up against a 1,200-pound horse or a 120-pound teenager?

The primary premise of this book is that there is not much difference. In a battle of wills, the average adult will *lose* to the horse or the teen *every* time! Most of us can accept that we will lose to the horse, which can so clearly overpower us. But we scratch our heads or lose our cool wondering how it is that the adolescent has us beat.

The good news, and the other premise of this book, is that there are effective ways to earn the cooperation of a horse or an adolescent—and those ways are profoundly similar. While effective, these ideas are not simple. In fact, many may seem counter-intuitive or paradoxical. They require one to rethink what is logical and to deal in abstract concepts. My hope and intention are to make those abstract concepts and that paradoxical thinking more natural for you to apply when interacting with the adolescents in your life.

This book is intended to offer a fresh perspective on adolescents and an innovative approach to reaching them. It is written for every parent, teacher, counselor, coach, or any other adult who interacts with teenagers on a regular basis and often feels confused or frustrated. My goal is to help you better understand and appreciate the various dynamics at play and to provide specific strategies for enhancing the relationships you have with the adolescents in your life.

The Origin of the Book and Its Principles

This book was actually born during my own adolescence. For many years, the highlight of each week was my Saturday riding lesson at Deerfield Riding Center in Great Falls, Virginia. When I arrived at the barn, I was assigned a horse to ride for that day, and it was my job to groom and tack the horse before the lesson. In the process, I not only learned to ride, I learned to work with, care for, and respect these powerful and complex creatures. I experienced a profound kinship with these wild and wonderful animals that I came to cherish deeply.

I quickly learned that the secret to a successful day of riding was to establish an element of trust that allowed for a collaborative relationship with my assigned horse. It seemed obvious to me that there was no way to get such a huge and powerful animal to do my bidding without its cooperation. Through trial and error, I learned that if the horse did not trust me, it refused to even consider the commands I gave.

Additionally, it became anxious and edgy and demonstrated this in a number of irritating ways: stomping a foot; pawing at the ground; pinning its ears back; swishing its tail; stopping short in front of a jump; refusing to walk, trot, or canter; or even running off and refusing to stop. In truth, a horse's anxious behavior could be more than irritating; it could be dangerous.

Likewise, if I did not trust my assigned horse, I became tense and anxious. I demonstrated this in ways that were different from my horse but equally problematic: tight reins, rigid posture, jerky movements, and other body language that was discernible to the horse. It was clear to me that to enjoy my day of riding, I needed to first establish a relationship with the horse, and the very core of that relationship had to be *respect.* Yes, not trust, but respect. As an adolescent with a keen eye and wise heart, I knew intuitively that the key to establishing trust was to establish respect. I knew that I was, in my own way, as powerful and complex a creature as the horse. And I knew I trusted only those who I truly respected.

The relationship between trust and respect, and the means for developing a mutually respectful relationship with such a powerful creature, came naturally to me as an adolescent. The inherent challenge in establishing such a relationship was one of the greatest joys and rewards of riding. But after college, as I began to work professionally with adolescents and was diligently trying to earn their trust in order to establish a therapeutic relationship, I temporarily forgot all the innate insights of my adolescent riding days. It was not until my mid-twenties, when I began to work with horses again, that the wisdom of my youth returned. I began to see ways in which my knowledge of horses informed and guided my understanding of adolescents. Indeed, I began to see how similar the two creatures really are.

PART I

Similar Creatures

The Striking Similarities Between Adolescents and Horses

Adolescents are much like horses, and I say this with a great deal of respect for both. Both are complex and beautiful animals, and both are often *misunderstood.* Horses are far more intelligent, perceptive, and intuitive than most people would ever dream. Adolescents, too, have far more to offer than we usually assume. Both have a great deal to teach us about ourselves, but we are usually so busy trying to teach *them* that we too often fail to learn the lessons they hold for us. Both adolescents and horses are fundamentally different from human adults, but we only recognize this in the horse. Our failure to recognize and appreciate the unique stage of adolescent development contributes immensely to our misunderstanding of adolescents and to the frustration that we feel toward them. It is also the root of their frustration toward us.

Both horses and adolescents are ***powerful***...not just in size but in will and determination. Since neither are members of the human adult world, they both have a natural tendency to be suspicious of and even distrusting toward adults. Their suspicion is, in many ways, a matter of survival. Horse herds have survived for centuries by trusting their natural suspicion of what is in their environment.

Likewise, in order for teenagers to mature into successful adults, they must learn to be independent. Finding their own way requires breaking away from the adult guidance of their childhood and striking out on their own. One fundamental task of adolescence is to begin to identify one's own values. To do so means to question the values previously presented to them. Although we often fail to recognize it, the suspicious and distrusting nature of either a horse or an adolescent is really nature's way of ensuring the survival of the species. It is a quality to be honored and respected, harnessed and guided, but not punished.

Both adolescents and horses are naturally ***curious***. When they are calm, relaxed, and engaged, this curiosity lends itself to learning or training. However, when they are tense or bored, their curiosity can lead to responding in ways that get them into trouble. Countless times I have heard from a teenager in trouble, "I just wanted to see what would happen." Unfortunately, for both horses and adolescents, their natural curiosity is paired with a very limited ability to think ahead to consequences. With this combination, it is no wonder many adults think that horses are dumb and teenagers are reckless. I assure you that neither is true.

Both adolescents and horses have a sixth sense for ***authenticity***. Horses sense when we are not being true to ourselves. They live only in the immediate moment. They are fully present and therefore not distracted by the past or the future. Their immediacy to the moment allows them to detect whether those around them are authentic or not. Adolescents have a similar sixth sense. I heard one teen refer to it as the "bullshit-o-meter." He was very articulate and colorful in his description of how he felt toward adults who were hypocritical, insincere, or phony. Most teens are not so colorful in their description and some may not even be cognizant of their intuition. However, all adolescents seem to have an uncanny ability to detect insincerity and, like horses, are repelled by it.

Both adolescents and horses readily experience ***fear***. For centuries, horses lived in wild bands on open ranges with many predators and few defenses. Where horses are allowed to remain wild, they continue to enjoy the precarious and fragile existence that comes with freedom. They feel vulnerable much of the time and rely heavily upon one another for mere survival. A heightened vigilance for safety is engrained in their species and remains a strong instinct even among domestic horses. Adolescents naturally experience the fear associated with the ominous task of becoming independent. They must leave the security of home and venture into the unknown in order to one day be secure adults. It is a paradox and a challenge, and just because each of us has done it successfully does not diminish the task in any way. For each teen, the task looms large and is occasionally overwhelming. For either the horse or the adolescent to *not* feel some fear would be foolish and unnatural.

Both adolescents and horses seek to find qualified ***leadership*** in their lives. Most teens won't admit this, but it is true. They easily feel insecure and long to find true leadership that they can trust. But both horses and teens instinctively understand that true leadership is hard to find and false leadership can literally lead them astray. So while they long for leadership, they are also highly suspicious of it. In ways that are strikingly similar, horses and adolescents "test" the would-be leaders in their lives to determine if they are worthy of respect and trust. Once you have earned their respect, and ultimately their trust, you can enjoy a reliable level of cooperation from them.

As you can see, both adolescents and horses present a number of similar and enthralling paradoxes. Both are strong and powerful, yet fearful. Both are naturally curious and inherently suspicious. Both are genuine and demanding of authenticity. Both are far more complex than most people assume. Both will challenge your mind and capture your heart, if you let them.

The Mistakes We Make

Most of us make a lot of innocent errors in working with horses. Fortunately, most horses are naturally forgiving and will allow us to correct our mistakes. Depending on the type and size of the mistake, we may need to spend some time repairing the relationship, but ultimately, we can return to a productive partnership.

Adolescents vary in their capacity to forgive the mistakes we make in our interactions with them. I have found most teens to be extremely forgiving of those who they've already identified as a trusted adult. Depending on the type and the size of the mistake we make, *and* our own ability to acknowledge and address our mistake, we may still be able to establish a strong and trusting relationship with the adolescent, even if that trust has not already been earned. However, I have also found that most teens are not at all forgiving of what they perceive to be our overall lack of understanding. Many of them correctly conclude that adults "just don't get it," and we are written off for our lack of insight and compassion. In truth, many adults do *not* understand and appreciate the unique dynamics of the adolescent stage of human growth and development. A lack of understanding leads to incorrect assumptions and insensitivity to the challenges they face. When mistakes are made innocently and we are willing to learn, most teens will forgive us for our misjudgments. However, we must be open to developing a better understanding and correcting our erroneous thinking. By picking up this book, you have already shown a willingness to do so.

The most significant error we make, and one that will be addressed throughout this book, is in viewing adolescents as small adults. They may look physically mature, and they often insist that they "don't need to be treated like a kid," but this does not mean they are adults. There is still a great deal of maturing to be done. Both their brains and their internal organs continue to develop long after their shoes size stops growing and they reach their full height. By expecting them to act like adults, to consistently show organization and good judgment and apply rational reasoning skills to important situations, we essentially set up the divide that then frustrates us. This is perhaps the most fundamental error we make, because so many of the others stem from this erroneous perspective.

Another critical error that we make with adolescents is underestimating their "muscle." When you stand before a 1,200-pound horse and feel the incredible strength of its chest or legs, it is obvious that you must contend with its strength. The strength of an adolescent is less obvious and better disguised, but still presents a force to be reckoned with.

The muscles of an adolescent are fueled by factors inherent in their unique stage of development. The physical and hormonal changes taking place in their bodies provide a powerful source of energy. Their natural drive toward independence acts much like a steroid, enhancing their will and determination to an almost unnatural level of strength. It is no wonder that to most adults, a stubborn and angry adolescent is just as scary and hard to control as a 1,200-pound horse.

The natural factors governing the unique stage of adolescent development are, in and of themselves, wonderful and essential components of our teenagers. Their surging hormones will help them develop physically into the adult men and women that we want them to become. Their powerful drive toward independence *can*, if not misdirected, help them become the capable and self-sufficient adults we long for them to be. The problem is *not* in the powerful forces driving their development. The problem is that as adults, we fail to fully understand their stage of development. We fail to appreciate the physical, social, and emotional challenges they face.

Perhaps we have forgotten our own adolescent years and the confusion, loneliness, or turmoil that we may have experienced as our bodies changed, our friends became painfully important, and our parents seemed like aliens. Or perhaps we remember it all too clearly and wish to spare our own teenagers from the distress we suffered. Perhaps we feel that we can somehow guide them so they don't repeat the mistakes we made. If we have forgotten, we need to remember that the stage of adolescence is fraught with challenges that would seem insurmountable to anyone caught in the abyss that lies between childhood and adulthood. And if we wish to spare them, we need to realize that each person must traverse that abyss in their own way in order to truly reach adulthood.

Even if we recall clearly the painful adjustment of our own teen years, we cannot possibly absorb the full impact of growing up in a world that is significantly different from the one in which we were raised. Teenagers today are growing up in an age of global terrorism, exposed to the graphic images of war and destruction. The falling of the Twin Towers and multiple school shootings are events of their generation. Political corruption of unprecedented proportion and growing awareness of the frailty of our planet are common topics of discussion. Theirs is the first generation to have television, the Internet, and many other forms of social media by which they gain immediate awareness of local and world events paired with graphic and memorable images. News is so readily available that even the most diligent parent cannot censor the information their child obtains.

The world around them is *not* safe. Most of us would not allow our kids to play unsupervised outside, as we enjoyed doing when we were kids. Today's children are taught at a very young age to be wary of strangers and they receive little or no physical affection outside of the home, as adults today are reticent to even offer a hug in an era of accusation and litigation. Most of the adults reading this book would agree that this is not the world we grew up in. It is a very different world that we encounter today, one that we navigate using the experience and coping skills of an adult. And even so, it still is often overwhelming for us. How much more so, then, must this unsafe world overwhelm our adolescents?

We wonder why they seem reckless or sullen and why so many seek the security and protection of neighborhood gangs or crews. We truly fail to honor the immensity of their task. Instead, we respond with frustration when they mouth off, cop an attitude, or seem apathetic toward things that are important to us. Underneath the exterior, most teens are frightened and doing the best they can with the skills they have to face a world that is truly unpredictable. The vigor and venom with which they often greet their world is, in fact, a quality that will help to preserve and protect them. But instead of appreciating that and honoring it, we resent it and want them to simply be the good children they were yesterday or the mature adults they will be tomorrow. They cannot do either. They *must* contend with their stage of development…and so must we.

The next error we make with adolescents is in trying to communicate with them in *our* language. Most of us would never expect a horse to understand the words we use. We know and appreciate that they have their own language, their own set of values and beliefs, their own priorities, and their own way of thinking. We accept without question that the horse thinks differently, holds different values, and speaks a language different from our own. However, somehow when we look at a teenager, we assume that since they are of our species, they must speak our language, hold similar beliefs and values, and think the same way we do. We certainly do not expect that they will always *agree* with us, but we do expect that they will think in a similar manner. How wrong we are!

Brain research in the last few years has confirmed what many parents have long suspected. Our teenagers are not as mature as they would like us to believe. But I mean this literally. Their *brains* have not yet matured. In the past few years, research based on PET scans (positron emission tomography) and fMRI (functional magnetic resonance imaging) has proven that the teenage brain is still very much under construction. While certain areas are well developed, such as those that govern motor control and hand-eye coordination, others will continue to develop for several more years. Because the adolescent brain is still developing, it is fundamentally different from the adult brain in a number of significant ways[1].

The prefrontal cortex is the area of the brain that governs executive function and thereby influences the way we organize, plan, develop strategy, and control impulses. It is separate and distinct from the areas of the brain that govern intelligence. The prefrontal cortex is not fully developed until the mid-twenties for girls and even later for boys[2].

Perhaps this sheds some meaningful light on the disorganized backpacks and lockers containing moldy lunches that frustrate parents and teachers of highly intelligent kids. As a school administrator, I advocated for regular "locker clean-up days." Many teachers protested that supervising teenagers to clean up their lockers took valuable time away from classroom instruction. I argued that helping our students develop organizational skills was every bit as important as the academic instruction being delivered in the classroom.

1. Judith Newman, "What's Really Going On Inside Your Teen's Head?" The Washington Post Parade Magazine (28 November 2008).
2. Ibid.

Some teachers questioned my logic until they discovered for themselves the value of checking lockers. Often, we found several weeks' worth of completed homework at the bottom of a messy locker or a half-finished English essay under a smelly gym uniform. We frequently discovered that our students were doing and learning more than their organizational skills allowed them to demonstrate without our help.

In addition to development of the prefrontal cortex, dopamine levels are not in full throttle in adolescence. Dopamine is a brain chemical that assists the brain in recognizing those things that are of critical importance and prioritizing them relative to the many other competing demands on our attention[3]. The difference in dopamine levels is what allows an adult to pay the utility bill and wait to purchase the desired new jacket, while the teenager spontaneously spends his entire allowance on Chinese takeout and ends up with no money for the movie he has been waiting all week to see.

Brain development is also at the root of the emotional impulsivity that many adolescents demonstrate. Research has shown that in reading facial expressions, voice intonation, and other social cues, adults and adolescents rely on different areas of the brain. Adults utilize the frontal cortex, which allows them to assess social situations from a perspective of reason, while adolescents utilize the amygdala, which immerses them in emotion while assessing social situations[4].

Given that teens assess social situations from a place of

---

3. Ibid.

4. Judith Newman, "What's Really Going On Inside Your Teen's Head?" The Washington Post Parade Magazine (28 November 2008). "Teenage Brains; Beautiful Brains," National Geographic (October 2011).

strong emotion and have little ability to prioritize, strategize, and think beyond the immediate moment, we can begin to understand that to a teenager a social mishap can seem cataclysmic, life altering, or devastating. And their reaction to it, while still seemingly dramatic, can make a little more sense to us. If we can keep all these things in mind, we can then offer a little more empathy and perhaps in so doing, we can also gain a little more credibility so that our counsel in how to manage the situation is not so easily dismissed. Only by understanding how they think can we hope to have any influence at all.

The difficulty is that while their brains are not fully developed, their bodies may appear to be. This often presents an optical illusion in which we see before us a young adult. However, it is only an illusion. Their internal organs and minds are not yet developed. They are teenagers, caught between childhood and adulthood, in their own unique stage of development. They are truly not small adults. However, they are no longer children either. They are no longer in awe of the world around them. They no longer look to adults for answers and reassurance. A certain element of innocence has been lost and replaced with a healthy dose of skepticism. They question authority and the norms of their society in an effort to determine *for themselves* what is real and what is important to them.

While this aspect of adolescence is the one that most adults find challenging, it is also one of the most critical. Try to imagine our society without a measure of skepticism and the courage to question. If no one had ever questioned authority, the world would still be assumed to be flat, the

United States would not even exist, blacks would still be enslaved, and women would not have the right to vote. Thank goodness that we are a species who questions and thinks for ourselves. Thank goodness we are not afraid to try new things and to invent better ways of living. So why begrudge our teenagers, who are naturally prone to this way of thinking, of questioning the status quo?

Okay, let's be perfectly honest here...we begrudge our teenagers their tendency to challenge the status quo and defy authority because somewhere along the line, *we* became that authority and *we* assumed the job of preserving the status quo. It is only a slight overstatement to say that the continued success of our society, the ability to advance as a species, is almost diametrically dependent upon this inherent conflict established between adults and adolescents.

So, given this inbred struggle, how can we ever hope to establish a collaborative relationship with our adolescents? The answer lies in being willing to truly accept and even embrace their stage of development and then to honor and pass the "tests" they present to us.

It's Not Personal

There is no way around the "test." Before you earn the respect and trust of a horse or teen, you will have to endure some degree of testing. The tests will vary in difficulty and duration, and you may not even realize you are being tested, but you are! Although you cannot avoid the test, there are a few things that will make it much easier to endure. If you can accept a few fundamental facts about your horse or adolescent, your interactions will be much more pleasant and you may be able to expedite the test.

In working with horses, understanding that they are prey and not predators in the food chain is essential to understanding the way they react to things. Understanding that their eyes have the ability to see in an almost 360-degree radius but operate independently and do not easily integrate experiences from one side to the other is also key to effectively working with them. Learning to read the subtle, but significant, cues in their body language is imperative! And understanding how they think and what is important to them can make all the difference in the world. There are many excellent natural horsemen (and women) who have written extensively on this topic, and a recommended reading list is included at the back of this book.

In the natural order of things, horses are prey that forage for food and humans are predators who hunt for theirs. Prey animals are instinctively wary of predators. Despite thousands of years of domestication, horses instinctively operate from a place of natural suspicion of all humans. We don't take that personally. We accept it as part of the difference in our species, and whether we use old methods or the new more natural horsemanship, we incorporate this natural difference into the way we work with horses.

In the past, we trained horses by overpowering them. The methods were cruel and unnecessary. A trained horse was called "broke." Thankfully, our methods have evolved as we have gained a greater understanding of horses. Natural horsemen and women no longer use barbaric methods to tame horses. The old ways have been replaced with more gentle methods that still incorporate the horse's natural prey mentality. But now we move with compassion to establish a relationship based on proving that we do not intend to hurt them. We aim for partnering with them; for establishing respect, trust, and cooperation...the very things we want in our relationship with our teenagers.

In working with horses, earning trust and respect and being accepted as a worthy leader is called achieving "join up." Among those adults befuddled by adolescent behavior, and feeling thwarted while trying to earn their cooperation,

I have heard more than a few exasperated adults use expletives and colorful language to describe their experience. Many parents have told me that they are not even hoping for a *good* relationship, they merely want to *survive* the teen years. They complain that there are no handbooks or cheat sheets available to guide them to better understand their teen. I will leave the horse training to those more qualified than I, but rather, will focus my efforts here on helping you understand a few things about teenagers that can forever change the way you approach them and maximize your potential for "join up."

To achieve partnership with our teens, we need to change our thinking about how we work with adolescents, in a similar manner to how we have changed the way we work with horses. We need to allow our growing understanding of adolescent biology and development to inform our methods of interaction. When we do, it is easier to avoid *taking things personally*. We can then come to understand that our teenagers are not *intending* to hurt us. Their attitude and behavior are fleeting and governed by an internal process as natural to them as the prey mentality is to the horse.

The most important thing for us to understand as we engage with our teens is that most of what adolescents do is driven by natural forces. Adolescent behavior is so largely governed by the hormonal changes taking place inside them that much of their behavior is somewhat beyond their control. The mood swings, the sullenness, the apathetic attitude…none of these is personal. Taking things personally is among the biggest mistakes we make in dealing with our teenagers. When we take their behavior personally, we lose all perspective. We forget that they are not small adults, and we n as we would to a neighbor or colleague who ame level of disrespect. We generally lose our cool and end up escalating the situation. I am not suggesting that we condone their behavior, simply that we cannot take it personally. To do so is as erroneous as assuming that a horse would want to hurt a human.

Once we truly and deeply accept this premise, we can begin to incorporate a number of other concepts and strategies that will further alter and improve our interactions with adolescents. The primary task of the stage of adolescence is to individuate. To accomplish this, they must separate from their parents. Their brain, their hormones, their very being is wired toward this ultimate goal. To say that it is a primal drive is not an exaggeration. View their behavior and attitudes through a lens that truly sees this primal force at work and it becomes easier to not take things personally while being more creative in the ways in which we interact with our teens.

Let's take a look at some of their "primal" behaviors. The first is related to their biology. The same hormonal changes that affect their shifting mood also affect their biological clock. It is a fact, for which there is significant scientific support, that the adolescent biological clock is set to be more nocturnal than diurnal. So when your teen wants to stay up late on Saturday and sleep all afternoon on Sunday, don't assume that this is her way of getting out of going to church or synagogue with the family. Don't immediately assume he is doing drugs or sneaking out of the house. An adolescent's natural biorhythm would prefer to be up at night and asleep during the day. Accept this. Acknowledge it. Don't take it personally. And help your teen understand that the world we currently live in is not designed to accommodate this. High schools all across the country have start times that make the average rooster yawn.

If asked, I would advise that schools start later...teens would get more sleep and be more alert in school. In addition, the sleep obtained in the early morning hours has proven to be important to brain development. So if schools started later, not only would teenagers get more sleep, they would get the important sleep that supports brain development. Additionally, they would get out of school later and have less time to hang out and get in trouble before parents who work outside the home return to provide supervision. But, alas, I have not been consulted on this important national scheduling issue. However, even without my consultation, several school districts have wisely applied this new research to their school start times and begin high school later. I applaud these forward-thinking school districts and hope that others will follow suit.

If you are not fortunate enough to live in one of these more progressive school districts, as a parent you have a responsibility to help your teenager get to school on time. I know that in 90% of the families I work with, getting the teen up in the morning is a topic of *huge* contention. Many families report significant battles over this. Understanding that your teen has a *biological* reason for the extreme difficulty in getting up will not eliminate the struggle but will alter your own perception of it and help you be more patient and understanding. Patience and understanding go a long way with a groggy, cranky teen!

Similar to the adolescent nocturnal nature, is their unusual internal clock. Although I have absolutely no hard data or scientific research to substantiate my claim, I will tell you this: adolescents have a different concept of time than adults do. Take for example the very minor requests that we make of one another. An adult asks another adult to hand them something and they do it…right away if possible. When asked to hand you something, your teen is likely to say "sure" and then continue texting, playing their video game, or reading their book. Their behavior seems both rude and intended to annoy. Yet when I talk to teens about this very issue, they seem perplexed, as if they have no idea that they should have complied with this simple request as soon as possible. Usually they shrug, and in their eyes I can see the very common thought, "Damn, these adults are UPtight!" It's the same when a parent asks an adolescent to clean up their room. The parent usually feels that a sense of timeliness is implied and assumed. But to the adolescent there is no such sense of time.

As adults, we can save ourselves a lot of aggravation and struggle with our teens if we can learn to speak in terms of their language and understanding of time. I find it most effective to be as clear *and* as flexible as is possible in any given situation. So, I might tell a teen that I want them to clean their room and then ask them when they think they will be able to do this. When they give me the typical "later," I do not get irritated and conclude that they are trying to get out of this chore…I accept it as part of their schema on time. I tend to gently push for a more definitive response by saying something such as, "Do you think you can get to it today?"

To help them structure their time and understand why I am concerned about when they are going to take care of this responsibility, I might remind them of other upcoming events or constraints to their time. It is also helpful to "contract" with them regarding something that makes sense to them and fits into their reference of time. So I might say, "Well, I know you want to watch football with your friends tomorrow. So, let's agree that your room needs to be clean by the time you want to leave...and if it's not you can just *start* then and join your friends when your room is finished."

Now, don't misunderstand me...I am not naïve. The teen will typically agree to this arrangement because it seems very reasonable and because the football game tomorrow seems like a lifetime away. They *feel* like they have all the time in the world. And when the game is ready to start and their room is not clean, they will try to engage you in a new deal. If you hold firm, they are likely to conclude that you are unreasonable and inflexible and even the "meanest parent in the world." So, before it gets to that point, try reminding them the day of the game that they need to clean their room before they leave. Even let them know how many hours they have remaining to complete this task. Try your best to say it with a helpful tone so as to not be accused of "nagging."

Adolescents are *extremely* sensitive to the perception that someone is micro-managing them, and you do run that risk. I suggest, however, that you take your chances, reminding them of their responsibility and simply bracing yourself for the possibility that they will resent your effort to help them. Be sure to spare yourself the headache of taking it personally, assuming that they are intentionally ignoring or defying your request. I assure you—they are not.

As previously mentioned, the primary task of adolescents is to individuate. Along with their natural drive toward independence, adolescents are also naturally infused with a strong desire for risk and adventure. The maturity and responsibility of adulthood is beginning to emerge, but often seems well concealed. They are *not* adults yet, and it is unfair of us to expect them to behave accordingly. As adults, we know from our own life experiences that certain situations are either dangerous or a dead end. And often we want to spare them the need to learn life's harsh lessons on their own.

Wouldn't it be wonderful if we could plug in a flash drive and just "download" all of the lessons they need to safely navigate the world? Ah…it's nice to dream, but we need to come back to reality. Our experiences are what make us who we are. They build character and define our values. None of that can be downloaded. Adolescents need and deserve an opportunity to experience the world in their own way and to learn for themselves the lessons that will help determine who they'll become as adults. Therefore, as adults, we need to recognize that it is *our issue* and not theirs that leads us to want to protect and guide them and makes it difficult for us to let go and let them venture out.

Approaching your adolescent with a deep appreciation for their primal drive toward independence, a firm grasp of the fact that they tick to a different clock, and a true acceptance that they are wired to seek experiences that will allow them to grow and develop, will not help you avoid the "tests" they create. However, it will most certainly help you avoid some of the frustration and angst that you feel when you engage with them. And I guarantee that approaching a teen (or a horse) with a genuine appreciation and understanding for the way they operate will expedite the testing process and lead to a more harmonious relationship.

Passing the Test

In any exchange with horses or adolescents, one must expect a certain degree of "testing." Remember that their natural position is one of suspicion. To follow the wrong leader is dangerous and to ensure that one is a worthy leader, there will invariably be tests. This testing can take the form of passive refusal or outright defiance. It can be done overtly, with a spirit of challenge, or it can be done covertly, with a spirit of disrespect. The tests can be delivered with playfulness or with hostility. Learning how to pass the various tests is essential to a congenial relationship with horses or adolescents.

An important component of passing the test is to understand and appreciate it. Recall that horses and adolescents are looking for leadership. In a certain way, they *want* you to earn their respect and trust. They *want* to relax and let you guide them gently. However, trust is a difficult thing for most of us, and for horses and adolescents trusting the wrong leader can have disastrous results. Therefore, they wisely require that you *earn* their respect and trust. When viewed in this way—as part of an intelligent means for assessing leadership—the test is not nearly so irritating and bothersome. It is not an assault on one's authority, but a means for validating it. In fact, at this point in my career, I have grown to welcome the test as a sign that I am being considered for leadership in an adolescent's life. What an honor! What a privilege! It motivates me to "study" for the test and strive to not only pass but pass with flying colors.

In my role as an administrator of a small private school for students with learning and emotional disabilities, I offered training at the start of each school year. I warned our new teachers, and reminded those who had worked with me before, that the *job* of an adolescent is to test the adults in their lives. I emphasized that it is *our* job to pass the test, and I handed out a "cheat sheet," inviting them to keep the cheat sheet handy in their classroom, to memorize it, and refer to it whenever they needed. I assured them that regardless of the form of the test (be it passive or defiant, playful or hostile) the best way to "pass" was to keep in mind what I call the 7 C's. The 7 C's involve being Calm, Clear, and Confident, while giving Choices and Consequences with Consistency and Compassion.

The First Three C's: Calm, Clear and Confident

Horses are exceedingly sensitive to energy. They sense even subtle changes in their environment. When people around them are anxious or agitated, horses pick up this tension and it makes them nervous. Remember that we are naturally predators who hunt for our food and horses are naturally prey who are hunted by cougars and other large cats in the wild. On some instinctive level, horses assume that if the predator among them is anxious, then things must be *really* bad. For this reason, one of the first things one learns when working with horses is that you must be able to manage your emotions and calm your energy when you're around them. A similar principle is at play in our interactions with adolescents...especially if there is any level of confrontation or disagreement at hand.

Therefore, first and foremost, when you sense you are being tested, remain CALM. Losing your cool or getting flustered by the test only exacerbates the situation by telling the adolescent that s/he has succeeded in causing you irritation, doubt, embarrassment, fear, or frustration. As soon as you lose your composure, you fail the test. By remaining calm, you communicate that despite what the teen is doing, you are in control of your own emotions. There is a powerful message in that level of control that will ultimately inspire respect and trust from the adolescent in a way that is very similar to a horse.

But let's be real! No matter how much yoga or meditation we may be doing, we cannot always be calm. There are times when we *will* feel irritated, embarrassed, or frustrated with our teenager. So what do you do when you do *not* feel calm? The trick is to recognize and admit to yourself that you are not calm and try to regain composure as quickly as possible. Start by taking some deep breaths. It is medically proven that taking a few deep breaths lowers one's heart rate, which in turn produces a calming effect. It is constitutionally impossible to remain as agitated after a few deep breaths as you were beforehand, given that the breaths are taken with the full intention of calming oneself.

However, sometimes even deep breaths just don't cut it! Depending on the initial state of arousal and agitation, a few deep breaths may not leave you calm enough to effectively begin to deal with the situation. You may want to wait and address the situation later, when you have had a chance to calm yourself. Any experienced horse trainer knows that when they feel agitated with the horse, it is time to take a break. And you may want to seek outside support in handling a situation that is escalating in intensity. Most novice horsemen and women hire trainers to help them work with their horses instead of taking the risks inherent in trying to handle things beyond their level of knowledge or comfort.

It is interesting to me that many adults report the feeling of partial defeat when they wait to address a problem situation with a teen. In actuality, the exact opposite is true. It is a very powerful position to take. It demonstrates that you are in control enough to make a logical decision. It puts the teen in the position of having to wait for an outcome. It gives you time and space to think the situation through. And it gives the teenager time to calm down too. Almost without exception, the discussion that occurs sometime *after the fact* is much more productive than the argument that would have occurred in the moment. Don't ever be afraid to say, "We will address this later."

Similarly, some adults are reluctant to request outside support in dealing with their teen, for fear that this will make them appear incapable of handling the situation. In truth, seeking outside support *is* one way of handling a situation, and it is a perfectly legitimate approach. Asking a counselor to meet with a student who seems depressed, or requesting the resource officer to pay a visit to your classroom where students are threatening and intimidating one another, shows that you are taking a situation seriously and are aware of your resources. It sets a powerful example that it is okay to go for help. It allows you to remain fully planted in *your* professional or parental role without getting pulled into areas beyond your expertise.

A parent who asks the school counselor to talk to their child about the effects of a recent divorce is not avoiding the painful dialogue with their teen, but acknowledging that their teen may find it easier to discuss their feelings with someone not directly involved. The parent or community that calls for police intervention in an unsafe situation demonstrates that adults are in control and will access the necessary resources to maintain safety. In many cases, bringing in outside support can actually *relieve* the parent or teacher from being in the role of enforcer and *alleviate* some of the tension in the adult-teen relationship. I have known many parents who, though reluctant at first to pursue juvenile probation for a wayward teen, eventually came to appreciate that the probation officer assumed the role of the "heavy," allowing the parents to return to the role of supporting and encouraging their teen in more positive ways.

So, do not ever be afraid or reticent to seek outside *professional* supports when a situation begins to feel out of control or outside your level of comfort and expertise. I should emphasize here that I am suggesting outside professional support. I am not suggesting that you ask neighbors, other parents, or other adults to "talk some sense into" your teen. I've seen too many times how this approach can backfire and end up actually undermining the parent's authority.

When being tested by a horse or a teen, the second principle is to be CLEAR in what you want. If the request is not clear, then the response cannot be judged as wrong. Being clear means being concise and direct. When an adolescent tests an adult, they often enjoy a high level of adrenaline. This adrenaline interferes with their ability to process complex information or to think abstractly. In such a state of arousal, there is no sense in trying to engage in debate or to convince them of your point of view. Usually, this is not the time to appeal to their rational side or to try to draw upon the positive relationship you usually enjoy. During the test, you need to be clear and focused. Give simple and direct instructions. We will look at an example shortly.

It is also very important to convey CONFIDENCE throughout the test. For new teachers, or parents just beginning to experience their adolescent's testing, this often involves a bit of "fake-it-till-you-make-it." Confidence is what conveys leadership, and as we discussed earlier, horses and adolescents are wired to test the would-be leaders in their lives to find those who are trustworthy. Confidence along with clear directives and a calm demeanor is what will ultimately earn respect and cooperation.

Calm, Clear, and Confident—sounds simple, heh? But let's be honest, when we are facing a stubborn horse or a defiant teen, we feel anything *but* calm, clear, and confident. So…how do we pull this off? What do these principles look like in real life?

Let's take an example. As a high school teacher, a student in your classroom is off-task. You have tried ignoring the behavior, but it has escalated. The student has begun to talk to other students, and when you request his attention, he mouths off to you and causes further disruption. You have tried numerous ways to set limits and redirect his attention—all to no avail. You begin to feel that you are losing control of the class, and you determine that you need to ask this student to leave your classroom. The student refuses.

At this point, most of us begin to get rather flustered… even enraged. Many of us are tempted to begin to engage in a dialogue that includes a combination of bribery and threats.

We often begin to lose our professionalism. Some primitive part of us may even begin to think things like, "I don't care if I *do* lose my job…I am gonna smack this punk." Hopefully, long before you get to this point, you are taking deep breaths and practicing the art of "fake-it-till-you-make-it." But since you have given a plain and clear direction—to leave the classroom—you can no longer exercise the option of waiting to deal with this student later. You are now in the position of having to enforce your authority in some manner. The best way to do so is to simply make clear your request. It is amazing how effective it can be to simply restate your request…with confidence and authority.

Confidence is the key. The confident manner in which you convey your request sends a very subtle, but powerful, message that you *know* you will prevail. Often this subtle message is enough to move the adolescent out of their position and into compliance. If you can remain calm—keeping your voice even and your speech slow and deliberate—and you can remain clear—repeating your expectation with the confidence of authority—you are likely to discover that the adolescent tires of trying to agitate you and complies with your direction to leave the classroom.

However, there are some teens who simply want to "up the ante" and see what happens if they defy further. This is where choices and consequences become important.

Continuing with the 7 C's: Choices and Consequences

Life is full of choices and each choice carries a consequence or a result of some kind. For horses, the "choice" is ultimately to cooperate or not. And when using more natural training methods, the consequences we apply boil down to "applying pressure" or "releasing pressure." Horses are highly peaceful animals, and they do not like pressure. They will respond to even the slightest pressure generated by a human's focus and energy. Increased pressure might be just an increase in energy or a slight movement toward them. To reward a horse for cooperating, we simply need to release the pressure by "backing off" from the request or giving them a break from being the focus of attention.

For teens, the choices we present seem much more complex and the range of consequences is expansive. But in many ways, the principles are the same. It is important to present adolescents with CHOICES whenever possible (and it is almost *always* possible). This may seem a little contradictory.

A minute ago I said that you need to give clear and direct instructions and now I am saying that you need to offer the ornery teenager who is testing you a choice?! Remember that earlier I warned you—these principles, though highly effective, are not exactly obvious. This particular principle is rooted in an understanding and respect of the unique stage of adolescent development. Adolescents have a deep need to feel in control. They need to feel that they are making their own decisions and are in charge of their own lives. How many times has your teen said things like, "Yeah? Make me!" or "You are not my boss!" or the two all-time teen favorites, "So what?!" and "Who cares?!"

Remember when I said that we don't really speak their language? If you or I, as adults, said those things to one another, it would have to emerge from a place of great disrespect, frustration, or defeat. When an adolescent says these things, it stems from a place of fear that they are not going to be able to one day take control of their own lives. It is a desperate attempt to demonstrate independence when they feel completely inadequate to the challenge. By the time an adolescent truly feels independent, they no longer utter these kinds of statements...they don't need to. Hence, the principle of offering them a choice.

By offering them a choice, we acknowledge that they are powerful and reassure them that they are still in control of some things in their lives. The reality is that there is *always* a choice. The trick for us as adults is to recognize and accept that they *do* have a choice and that what they say is true—we *can't* make them. Long gone are the days in which they were small enough to pick up and physically put in "time out" if they refused when asked. Once we accept this simple but humbling fact, then we can begin to master the art of designing choices at critical junctions. Here, the key is to offer two choices and to *genuinely* be able to accept their selection of either one.

Most of the time, we will have a natural preference for one of the choices, and that is fine. We can even tell the adolescent that we hope they will choose X. However, we cannot be *so* invested in the adolescent choosing X that they want to choose Y simply to defy us. We must develop some level of detachment from the decisions they make. Often the adolescent will choose Y without intending to defy us, and we can warn them that we think it is a poor choice. We can even encourage them to rethink the situation and make a better choice. However, ultimately we *must* respect their choice and let the "chips fall where they may." To do anything else disempowers the teenager, who will respond by exerting power in ways that can be problematic or even dangerous.

Allow the CONSEQUENCES to unfold. For many parents, and even teachers and therapists, this is the hardest part. Once the adolescent has made their choice, we *must* allow the consequences to flow from their decision…otherwise, it was not a real choice, and in the next interaction our adolescent will no longer have reason to believe that we mean what we say. If we don't "mean what we say and say what we mean," we have no integrity. And without integrity, the adolescent cannot respect and trust our leadership.

So, let's return to our disruptive and defiant adolescent who refuses to leave the classroom when instructed to do so by the teacher. Our calm, clear, and confident demeanor has not worked in eliciting the teen's cooperation. We now need to engage the principles of choice and consequence. If we are truly calm and thinking clearly, it is much easier to design our choice. However, it may take a minute or two to recognize that there *are* two options that we *can* live with. The two options we can live with become the choice we present to the adolescent. So, in this instance, I might say, "Your choice is to leave my classroom on your own or I will need to call the principal to come and escort you out of my classroom." By the way, the use of "my classroom" repeated twice in the above statement is intentional and serves to further reinforce my confidence and authority…and might contribute to the teen making a choice to leave on his/her own.

If the teen does *not* leave on his/her own, remember that they are *testing* you. And this is the moment of truth. You *must* now call the principal to have the student escorted out of your classroom. You *cannot* fail to follow through on your own choice. To fail to follow through is to fail the test altogether. And you can be certain that the next choice you give will have little to no credence if you are not willing to follow through. For this reason, it is critical that you only present choices you are willing and *capable* of following through with. Idle threats can seem tempting, but in my experience will backfire almost every time.

Now, let's say that you work in a large school and calling the principal is not a real option. Then, by all means, do *not* offer this as one of the choices. An alternate and effective choice in this case might be the following: "Your choice is to leave my classroom on your own or to remain in the classroom by yourself and I will remove the rest of the students to the cafeteria to continue our lesson. If you want to inconvenience your peers in that way, that's your choice." Most teenagers will not inconvenience an entire class simply to make their point. And offering them this choice also provides them a means of "saving face." They can now leave your classroom, *not* because you asked them to do so, but because they do not want to infringe on their classmates.

Remember, that their supposed reason for leaving is entirely immaterial. The point is that you have managed to elicit their compliance without losing your cool (or your job) and you have demonstrated that you are an adult worthy of respect, in that you could handle and pass the "test." Do not be surprised if by year's end, this same student is one of your favorites and one who is most cooperative and seems to most clearly like you. By passing the test, you have earned respect...which will lead to trust...which will qualify you as a worthy leader in this adolescent's life.

But be warned, many adolescents offer multiple tests before they finally conclude that you are indeed worthy of their respect. For these students, the principles of consistency and compassion become critical.

The Final C's: Consistency and Compassion

Horses like consistency. They enjoy a rather predictable existence and can become easily unnerved by even small changes in their environment. At the same time, horses also enjoy a little variety. They are clever and interactive animals and can become ornery if bored by total routine. For this reason, horse trainers attempt to maintain a delicate balance of consistency and variation in a horse's training regimen. In a very similar manner, while adolescents enjoy variety, seek new experiences, and tend to want to explore new environments, they also need a certain level of consistency.

The principle of CONSISTENCY should be the easiest to follow, but it often seems to get adults into trouble. The rules (in your home, office, or classroom) need to be the same from one day to the next. The consequences for breaking the rules need to also remain the same. And household or classroom rules should apply to everyone in a similar manner. Now, granted there are logical exceptions and adolescents usually understand these. Older children have a later bedtime and high school seniors have more privileges than high school freshman. However, if a child in the family steals money from a parent, it should not matter which child it was—the consequence should be the same. If a student gets into a fist fight, it should make no difference if that student is a freshman or a senior. Consistency is a means of conveying order, constancy, and predictability. It allows horses and teens to feel safe by knowing what to expect.

Horses are so keenly aware of their environment, because in the wild their survival depends on it, that they notice even the smallest of changes. It is not unusual for a horse to "spook" at something as innocuous as a new tarp draped over some barn equipment. A teenager is unlikely to "spook" if the household furniture is rearranged or if the walls are painted a new color, but don't be surprised when they are more reactive than you expect. Change can be unsettling, so be considerate by being sensitive to their hyper-vigilance of their environment.

Consistency also encourages responsibility. If a teen knows the rules and the rules don't change, then breaking them is no one's choice but their own. On the other hand, if rules and expectations constantly change, adolescents—just like horses—feel anxious. The environment may seem to be unstable to them and thereby unsafe. Once you have established a procedure, structure, rule, or expectation…stick to it. It provides a base from which your adolescents are able to operate. Changing that base can be extremely unsettling, even if the change is for the better.

I have known many well-intentioned teachers who tried to make improvements in their class environment by establishing a new procedure. Parents are routinely tempted to implement something that seems to be working for another parent. It is certainly reasonable for any teacher to learn something in a workshop or from a more seasoned colleague and want to implement it within their classroom or for a parent to read about a new parenting approach and want to use it. The problem is that doing so carries a consequence and therefore needs to be done with forethought. If the importance of consistency is underestimated, even the most effective and well-intentioned teacher can unwittingly invite havoc into the classroom at the very time they are trying to improve it. And how many parents determine that a new parenting strategy doesn't work because they failed to implement the change thoughtfully?

So what should a teacher or parent do if they feel highly invested in establishing a new rule or procedure? If done thoughtfully, it *can* be done successfully. But it requires a delicate balance of timing and communication. The teacher or parent is well advised to wait until a natural time of change. Fortunately, the adolescent calendar is filled with these. A teacher can implement a new routine or policy at the start of a new quarter, semester, or school year. If the semester is too far off, then at the very least, wait until the start of a new month or a new academic unit. The parent can use the same school markers or wait until the end of a sports season or a birthday or holiday. The reason for this is simple. It makes more sense, and therefore, it feels safer. Change that does not make sense feels unsafe. And in response to feeling unsafe, adolescents and horses will sometimes react in extreme ways.

However, timing is only one part of the equation. There must also be communication. The teacher or parent who wants to change a rule or procedure needs to communicate *what* the change will be, *when* the change will occur, *why* the change is being made, and *how* the adolescents will benefit. They must be prepared to answer questions, hear rebuttal, tolerate some grumbling, and even offer some empathy to the teens who are unhappy with the change. A teacher is advised that communicating the same to the parents can reduce the influx of calls that will likely occur when students go home complaining about the teacher's new policy. Throughout all this, they must remain firmly resolute and committed to the new policy or expectation.

Either overtly or subtly, it is important for the parent or teacher to convey that they are not asking permission to change the policies in their own home or classroom. The new policy will be established, but they are giving the adolescents the time and information they need to adjust to the change. It is helpful to recognize that while all the energy is being directed at the new policy, the true energy is in response to the change. Any change can elicit such a reaction.

If the proper groundwork is laid, the new policy will be implemented more smoothly. However, once the change has been implemented, the parent or teacher should anticipate a period of time in which the children or students try to reverse the decision...or call for a "recount of the votes." This is simply the final test to ensure that the parent or teacher is as committed to her new policy as the *adolescents need her to be* in order to feel safe again in the new landscape of the classroom or home.

What is critical here is the understanding that all of this—the communication and the timing, the reaction and the need for you to remain resolute—is necessary in order for the adolescents to respect the adult and trust his/her judgment in establishing a new rule or policy. While rules or policies change, your demeanor does not. Continue to convey a clear sense of authority, respect for your adolescents, willingness to communicate, and sensitivity to their feelings. Ultimately, it is these aspects of your demeanor that will convey consistency amidst change. By being thoughtful about how and when to change a policy, you can convey consistency in these critical areas.

Before we leave the topic of consistency, I want to mention one of the most common pitfalls I see. Suppose that a student breaks a known rule. A well-meaning teacher, wanting to forge a better relationship with the student, talks openly with the student who eventually acknowledges their wrongdoing. The teacher, in an effort to be kind and flexible and solidify the relationship, lets the student off without the usual consequence. This well-intentioned attempt is likely to backfire. Remember that teenagers don't think the way we do. As an adult, if you made a mistake and your boss let you off the hook with a warning, you would feel lucky, grateful, and perhaps determined to never be in that situation again. Teenagers do not think that way. So the teenager, who was let off the hook with a conversation instead of the consequence they know they deserve, thinks that the teacher is "soft," inconsistent, easily manipulated, and not worthy of respect or trust. In trying to improve their relationship, the teacher has instead compromised it.

The final "C" is perhaps the most important. Above all, and throughout every interaction, show COMPASSION. While we are being calm and clear and confident, offering choices and enacting consequences consistently, we must always come from a place of genuine compassion. Remember that adolescents, like horses, have a sixth sense for authenticity. Therefore, our compassion cannot be artificial. True compassion is also not sugary sweet. Compassion is the genuine feeling of care for another—a deep sense of wanting to do what is best for the other. Adolescents *know* when you care. They pick up and respond to compassion with incredible sensitivity. In my experience, you can assign severe consequences (such as expelling a student from school) yet retain the respect and trust of the adolescent, if you are genuine in your compassion.

Let me offer an example of how the principles of consistency and compassion might look in the "real world." One of the most difficult decisions in my career as a school administrator was the decision to expel a student, who I will call Don. Don had almost completed a successful year of seventh grade at my school. However, toward the end of the year, his level of aggression began to escalate slightly. When Don did not get his way, he became defiant and disruptive. On one occasion, he lost such self-control that a physical restraint was required to keep him safe and ultimately the police had to be called to intervene. It was so close to the end of the school year, and he'd had such a successful year overall, that the decision was made *not* to expel Don, but to allow him to return the following year with the clear understanding that continued loss of self-control or aggression would be grounds for expulsion from our program.

The following school year, Don began by doing well. However, within the first two months, we started to see a similar pattern of defiance developing when he was frustrated. I warned Don and his parents that any aggression would result in dismissal from our program. My dilemma was that I *really* liked Don…and his parents, for that matter. Don had been adopted as a toddler and much of his learning and emotional issues could be traced to his days in an orphanage. He was also charming, funny, athletic, artistic, a hard worker, with a winning smile and a big heart. I really wanted Don to be able to remain at my school.

Unfortunately, the day came when Don's aggression exceeded what could be tolerated in our program. He was at home on suspension when I met with his parents to inform them that Don would no longer be able to attend our private school. They were devastated and distraught and wondered where he would be able to obtain an appropriate education that could address his learning and behavior issues. They also said they could not bear the idea of telling him this news. They anticipated that he would be equally distraught.

It was consistency (both with school policy and in my message to Don) that ensured I expel him. However, it was compassion that led me to offer to follow his parents to their home and deliver the news to Don myself, in his home where he felt most secure. In delivering the news to Don, I was straightforward but conveyed with sincerity how much

I cared about what happened to him. I explained to Don that he needed a school that could provide support for both his learning needs *and* his extreme anger and aggression. I reminded him that my school did not offer that kind of support for aggression. I told him that as sorry as I was to see him leave our school, I knew it would be best for him. I also told Don and his parents that I would be happy to assist them in the next step of their process to find an appropriate school program.

Don's parents were shocked at how well he took the news. I, however, was not so surprised. I knew that my compassion was sincere, that what I was doing was fair and had been forewarned—and it was truly being done for Don's own good. I trusted that all of that would come across in my communication, and it did.

Don went on to a number of alternative school placements before the right one was found, and I continued to work with him and his family in private therapy throughout each transition. I still see Don in my private practice, and at the time of this writing he is eighteen, has a driver's license, a part-time job, and is on the highest level of the behavioral program at his school. For Christmas this year, he gave me a huge coffee table book on horses! No matter what the situation demands, as a parent, a teacher, or another adult working with adolescents, if you exert compassionate authority with teenagers, they will trust and respect your leadership.

Parents have many opportunities to demonstrate consistency and compassion together. As long as we do not look at consequences as a way to "get back at them for bad behavior," we can enforce rules and still provide loving support. Take the teenage girl who breaks curfew knowing that the policy at home is that breaking curfew one week will lead to being grounded the next. The next week there is a big party that she has been looking forward to attending. Following through on the grounding is necessary, but it is not necessary for her to be entirely miserable all weekend. She misses the party, but perhaps she can have a friend over for a movie night. Or perhaps the parents offer to do something else she might enjoy. The compassion comes through when the consequence is simply something she earned by knowingly breaking her curfew. Let the consequence stand, but show compassion for her disappointment in missing the party.

A teenage boy takes the family car and is caught speeding. There has to be a consequence. Perhaps one was not previously established, and this is a great opportunity to invite the teenager's input for what the consequence should be. Acknowledging that there needs to be a consequence is showing consistency; allowing input shows compassion.

The teenager caught smoking or drinking alcohol under age presents parents with yet another opportunity. As long as you don't lose your perspective or blow your top, you can enforce a meaningful consequence in a compassionate manner. Perhaps you offer your teen the choice of either missing the next football game or an upcoming party. Let them know that instead of that event, you will be spending that time with them in discussion about the pros and cons of using nicotine and alcohol. During the discussion, empathize with the desire to try new things, to experiment, and to be a part of the crowd. Try to understand the situation from your teen's perspective. Listen to what s/he has to say. *Really listen.*

Resist the temptation to lecture. Recognize the adolescent's need to figure things out for themselves. And then agree on a clear consequence to be applied if s/he chooses to smoke or drink again.

Examples of Passing the Test

Because this concept of passing the test is so critical, and because the "test" can take so many different forms, I want to offer a few true-life examples in which I have changed the names but preserved the significant details. These represent only a small sampling of the myriad ways in which teens might test adults. As you read these examples, I predict you will recognize similarities to "tests" you've undergone yourself with the teens in your own life.

"Jim"

Jim was a senior at the school the year I arrived as the new Dean of Students. He had been fond of the previous dean and had no interest in getting to know me or any intention of coming to trust me. I was warned by several other staff members that Jim was a "hard nut to crack." I made an effort to forge a relationship with Jim, but he was consistently resistant—even quietly dismissive of me. However, as time went on, his resistance grew slightly more defiant, and I sensed he was "testing me."

The day finally came when he defied a specific and direct request. His defiance was very public, in the school hallway, and was over a rather basic school rule. There was absolutely no way for me to ignore his behavior or try to compromise with him. It felt a little like a stand-off or a showdown. I knew I could not win a battle of wills and had to offer him a choice. I also knew that both choices I offered had to reinforce my position of authority. So, I told him to comply with my original request or leave the school building. I reminded him that since he was eighteen years old, I had no legal obligation to allow him to be in my school if he was not going to follow school rules.

Jim was dumbfounded. He literally asked, with disdain and disbelief, "Are you serious?!" I replied as calmly as I could, "I am entirely serious. The choice is yours. Follow the school rules or leave the school building." He challenged me one more time with a sarcastic and hostile tone, "And what if I don't?" To which I replied calmly and with confidence, "Then you will be trespassing on school property and I will call the police to have you removed." Jim looked at me for a long minute, mumbled "this is bullshit," and left the school building.

Having stood firm in my position of authority, and having forced his compliance, I knew that I now needed to balance the relationship with compassion. Compassion looks different for each teen. I thought a lot about the best way to approach Jim the next time I saw him. I put myself in

Jim's shoes. As an older teen, in his senior year, he had lost a trusted adult—and I was the replacement for a person he had not wanted to lose. He did not want to forge a trusting relationship with me. The compassionate thing was to respect his position on that. I determined that Jim would likely want to return to school without being forced to dialogue about the previous day's events. After all, he had complied. I would not make a big deal about his initial defiance or his eventual compliance.

Jim returned the next day and neither one of us mentioned the incident. For the rest of the school year, I greeted him casually, offered him as much space as possible, and basically left him alone as long as he was not causing any problems. For his part, Jim never again defied my request. Often he complied in a slow and begrudging fashion, but he never again challenged my authority. A few days before he graduated, he came to my office to ask me a question, and as he left my office he said, "You know…you didn't turn out to be as bad as I thought you would be." I smiled and thanked him sincerely, knowing this was his way of acknowledging the respect and compassion that I had shown him over the course of the year and indicating that I had ultimately passed his test.

"Paul"

Paul was very different from Jim, and so was his style of testing. He offers a good example of how sometimes the test is subtle, non-confrontational, and even good-natured. It is, however, still a test.

Paul was a freshman when I arrived as the Dean of Students. He was a young man with a very troubled past. He longed for relationship and leadership but had good reason to distrust adults. He was playful in the way he tested me. On one occasion early in the school year, some students were having a get-together outside of school. The teaching staff had been invited and he asked if I was coming. I said I was not sure if I could. He badgered me playfully, saying that I *had* to come. As I wavered, he added with a grin, "If you ever want me to like you, you will come."

I was not sure why it was so important to Paul that I be there. He hardly knew me. But I sensed that it was an important "test," and that to pass it, I needed to attend the event. Many months later, as I got to know Paul and better understood his situation, I realized how rare it was for Paul to ask any adult for *anything*. He had come to accept that adults did not listen, did not care, and could not be counted on for even basic needs. They certainly could not be trusted to follow through on what they said. Simply asking me to come to the event had been a risk. And because he *wanted* me to pass the test, he gave me indicators that it was important. By listening to him and wanting to earn his trust, I had. The trust that I earned by simply going to this one school event served me well throughout my work with Paul for another three years, until he left our program to return to public school.

"Sam"

Sam's story provides the best example I can think of to illustrate the importance of conveying confidence in interactions with adolescents. Sam was a playful and mischievous young man. He had a great deal of underlying anger but masked it by being the class clown. He was not afraid to cause a ruckus in school and was willing to risk suspension to gain the attention and admiration of his peers. He had only been at my school for about three months, and most of the staff found him very frustrating. He certainly presented more behavioral issues than our average student. He seemed to have little regard for adults and an unquenchable thirst for peer attention.

One day, a stink bomb went off in the main school hallway and a terrible odor disrupted the nearby classrooms and interfered with learning for several hours. I immediately began to investigate the situation by asking teachers which students had recently been out of class and then questioning those students. Sam was on my list, and although he adamantly denied any knowledge of the prank, I *knew* he had been responsible. I had no proof whatsoever, but I knew it nonetheless.

Having ruled out all the other possible suspects, I returned to Sam with determination. In my second round of questioning Sam, I told him that although I would not reveal my source, I *knew* he was responsible for the prank. I told him that I would give him five minutes alone to consider his options. His first option was to continue to deny his involvement and force me into a more thorough investigation to find proof of what I already knew to be true. His second option was to "own up" to his prank and accept the consequences. I emphasized to Sam that there was a lot at stake in his decision.

I spoke with confidence and conviction in telling him that I absolutely knew he was responsible. I told him that in the next five minutes he needed to determine what type of relationship he wanted to have with me. He could be either a student who lied or a student who told the truth. If he owned up to his prank, I would be able to respect him as a student who could be honest. If he continued to deny his involvement until I found the proof I needed, he would forever be a student I didn't trust. I reminded him that he was already off to a rocky start with many of his teachers and that being a dishonest student in my book was not going to help him out much. As I left him alone in my office, I said firmly, "You have five minutes to think about whether you want to be an honest student in my school or a student who I *know* lies. Your choice."

I returned five minutes later and simply said, "Time is up. What's your answer?" Sam hesitated for only a second before blurting out, "I don't want to be a liar!" I nodded and thanked him, commended him for taking his first step toward being a more honest and upright member of our school community, and then sat down to talk with him about what we could agree upon as a reasonable consequence.

I wish I could say that Sam became a model student, but he did not. Sam continued to have significant behavioral difficulties in school, and most of his teachers continued to find his disruptive behavior extremely frustrating. Each time Sam was referred to my office, I firmly reminded him that he was a student who could be honest and that I was an adult who would be fair. And I also reminded him that trust could be destroyed by lying to me at any time. With that simple reminder, I continued to enjoy a relationship with Sam that allowed me to have confidence in our interactions.

"Wally"

Wally was a tall, skinny young man with glasses and an extremely tough exterior. When he was young, his father had mercilessly ridiculed him for being smart and enjoying reading. Eventually, Wally refused to read at all and developed the tough "red-neck" presentation he hoped would win his father's approval. However, his parents had split up after years of domestic violence, and his father was rarely in his life at the time when I met him.

Wally naturally had a high level of distrust for adults. He was aloof and contemptuous. He made most adults feel uncomfortable by his mere attitude—quietly non-compliant and clearly full of disdain. I worked hard to set consistent limits and be fair with Wally, hoping he would see me as a safe adult. I also tried, whenever possible, to honor any fair requests he had, in an effort to show him that I cared and could be an ally. However, his testing of me seemed relentless and unending.

Well into the school year, after several months of working with Wally but having not yet passed his test, he was caught smoking in the boys' bathroom. As a consequence, I decided he and I would watch an educational film on smoking during what would otherwise have been a recreational period for him. As I started the video, Wally put his head down on the desk in front of him, as though he was going to take a nap. Months of unrecognized effort mounted to the point of exasperation. I knew I had no way to "make" Wally watch the video.

Instead, I turned it off and spoke to him in an uncharacteristically sharp tone. "I really don't know what the **hell** you expect from me, but this thing is a two-way street. I want to advocate and support you, but you **gotta** give me something back. You were suspended only one day for smoking and part of the consequence is that you **watch this** video. I can't **make** you watch it, but I **can tell** you this….your **refusal** to watch this video is like a big 'F You' to me and to the school. If you continue to take that attitude and **never** offer **any** cooperation, you are **seriously** limiting the support that **I or this school** can offer you. It has been **months** of trying to work **with you** and you seem determined to sabotage the opportunity you have here and create an adversarial situation. I am willing to work with you, but I WILL NOT work harder than **you** are willing to work. **You got that?!"**

Sadly, Wally was rather accustomed to this kind of sharp tone, and for the first time, I seemed to make sense to him. He looked at me with a new kind of understanding—even appreciation. He didn't smile, he didn't respond, he simply picked up his head and looked in the direction of the video screen. I was a little wound up at that point and ready to continue with my diatribe. Fortunately, however, I took a deep breath and slowed my thinking. I realized that Wally's head being up and facing the video screen was a sign of cooperation. It was perhaps the first clear, outward, and genuine sign of cooperation he had ever offered me. I knew instinctively not to push for more—at least not at that time. I turned on the video, and we watched it together in silence. When it ended, I engaged him in questions from a guide and he participated—minimally, but he did participate.

That afternoon was a strange turning point. My relationship with Wally was forever changed. He remained quiet and aloof but grew more cooperative and, over time, more talkative. As time went on, I came to understand that what had eventually allowed me to pass Wally's test was my *genuine* expression of frustration. That I could feel *that* frustrated for not being able to connect with him somehow finally convinced Wally that my investment in him was real.

Wally had seen a lot of therapists and had come to believe we were all really "just in it for the money." He had also come to believe that we would all eventually give up on connecting with him, if he made it difficult enough. By allowing him to see that I cared enough to become truly frustrated in my thwarted efforts, Wally opened to the possibility that I might be a little different from other therapists he had seen. It still took many more months before Wally allowed himself to engage in therapy and begin to discuss some of the painful things that had created his tough exterior as a means of survival. Ultimately, however, we developed a wonderful working relationship that stymied many others in the school.

Wally continued to violate school and community rules, and he was never a model student, but he grew to show me respect by being honest with me, by listening to my counsel, by *sometimes* heeding my advice, and by being just a little less aloof. He taught me that sometimes the test is passed and respect is earned as the result of continued effort and authentic expression of feelings.

Wally's mother was an equally tough individual. Having survived abuse that would make most women timid, she was a fortress of determination. However, she was not at all clear on how to respond to Wally's defiance of home and community rules. When he got in trouble, she yelled and screamed and called him names, but enforced no meaningful and effective consequence. I tried for many months to help her see the importance of giving Wally limits and boundaries and remaining consistent in enforcing them. Knowing that Wally would not easily comply, she could not see the real value in the kind of effort that would be required.

One day, in exasperation at my failed attempts to help her understand the importance of providing limits for her son, I suddenly decided to try another tactic.

"You grew up on a farm," I said suddenly, seeming to change the subject entirely. She looked at me in a puzzled manner and nodded. "When you turn a horse out to pasture, what is the first thing it does?"

She thought for a minute and said, "It kicks up its heels."

"Right! And then what does it do?"

"It runs around," she stated with a tone that expressed doubt about where this discussion was heading.

"Exactly…it runs around…it establishes for itself the boundary of its pasture. It wants to know how far it can go. And if there is no fence, it will get anxious and keep on running. In truth, the horse does not want to be in an open space with NO boundary. It feels safer knowing the limits to its territory." I paused, wondering if she would begin to see the connection herself. Then gently, I said, "Your son is like a young horse turned out to a pasture. He is looking for the fence. You are giving him no clear fence and so he is continuing to run loose. He will not tell you with words that he wants a fence, but his behavior is repeatedly asking for you to establish one."

For the first time, Wally's mom seemed to understand that it was not an option but a parent's obligation to establish the rules, limits, and boundaries, and to enforce them. For the remainder of our work together, we continued to return to this analogy that proved helpful to her. She was the first to experience my perspective on adolescents being much like horses, and her response was validating. I will long remember, and hold dear, Wally and his mom.

Kindness is Weakness... But Muscle is Meaningless

Anyone who has ever led a horse knows that there is no sense in pleading with or trying to cajole the horse into cooperation. You will not earn a horse's cooperation just by talking softly and saying "please." The horse does not feel the need to return your kindness with kindness. In fact, the thought sort of makes us laugh. And yet, for many adults, there is a tendency to think that if we are simply **nice** to the adolescents in our life, then they will return our kindness with kindness.

This may be true to a point, and certainly, I am not advocating that you be mean or unfair to your adolescent, but it is naïve to believe that kindness is enough to earn cooperation. In fact, I will go one step further and suggest that for many horses *and* teenagers, kindness *alone* can be perceived as a form of weakness. If *all* you are is kind and loving, then you are not demonstrating the kind of strength and competence that the horse and teenager need in order to respect you and trust your leadership.

Many of us have seen the parent who tries to be her adolescent's "friend." This parent hopes that by being "hip" and "cool" and a "friend," her teen will like her and be cooperative. The problem is that teenagers need both friends *and* parents. They have an entire peer group to select from when choosing their friends. However, they only have one or two parents (or more if there are active stepparents involved). So they really need their parents to remain in the parental role. Invariably, being a child's "friend" backfires. The teen resents the attempt to be a part of his or her crowd and is embarrassed among friends who may see the parent as "cool" but not mature or responsible.

Most of us can clearly see the trap in trying to be a "friend" to an adolescent, and yet we easily fall into this trap in more subtle ways. We may try to share stories of our own adolescence in hopes of conveying that we understand. We may agree to keep a secret from another parent or teacher to show that we are more trustworthy and understanding than others. We may even look the other way while our teen and their friends drink or smoke pot in our basement or skip school, remembering the rules we broke when we were kids. All of these examples are a far cry from the parent who really tries to be a teen's "friend," and yet they are driven by the same desire to earn a teen's cooperation through understanding and connection.

The problem is that we forget that teens do not think the way we do. To adults, these gestures may seem like a way of connecting and showing patience and understanding. However, to the average teen, these things are simply a deviation from our adult role and they create confusion and a lack of respect for our ability to remain solidly and consistently in that role. We may be attempting to connect with our teen by allowing these infractions, but they simply see us as inconsistent, unpredictable, and therefore not deserving of respect and not worthy of trust.

On the other hand, in working with both teens and horses, I have seen that muscle is meaningless. It is easy to understand that your muscles are not impressive to a horse. Anyone who has ever worked with a horse, a 1,200-pound creature of muscle and will, knows that your aim is for collaboration and cooperation, not for compliance. You would be foolish to believe that you could get this animal to comply with your request, to submit to your authority simply because you are the human and he is the horse.

In a similar way, your muscle means very little to an adolescent either. Yet, how often do parents, teachers, and other adults demand the compliance of a teenager? How often do we say, "Because I said so!"? How often do we expect that they will submit to our request simply because we are the adult and they are the minor? In my opinion, it is as foolish to aim for the submissive compliance of an adolescent as it is to aim for the submissive compliance of a horse. Both are creatures of muscle and strong will. Most adolescents feel rather invincible and indestructible. Remember that their hormones and their drive for independence provide an almost unnatural level of will and determination. There is little you can do to intimidate an adolescent. And yet so many adults, especially men, try to take this approach in earning cooperation.

John was a headstrong and aggressive adolescent in the school where I was Dean of Students. I called in his parents for a conference to seek their support in helping John develop better ways to express his frustration. John's father arrived and was a towering man of solid muscle—a rather menacing figure. His response to my concerns was to reassure me that he would "take care of it." He had a strong military background and was clearly accustomed to "pulling rank" to elicit compliance. However, using this approach with John was simply inviting rebellion and aggression.

I began to realize that helping John would require helping his father to better understand that his son's developmental task was to develop his own independence and that John would do this even at the risk of a physical altercation with his father. It was not an easy endeavor. Although slowly, I helped John's father appreciate that his son had inherited his strength of conviction and his determination. I suggested that he could help his son develop these traits as he had done and learn to use them judiciously. I urged him to accept the challenge of earning John's cooperation through firm limits and the application of fair and compassionate choices and consequences. I asked him to relinquish the approach of intimidating John into submissive compliance.

Throughout the school year, there were numerous struggles between John and his father. John's father's military experience and years of relying on his physical prowess and rank were hard to let go of in parenting his son. However, John's father came to appreciate that "parent" is not a rank, but a role. It is a role that is most effectively played by establishing a relationship based on respect that leads to cooperation. He realized that for John to develop into a mature and responsible young man, he would need to develop tools beyond intimidating others into compliance, and he needed his father's example to do so. I do not think John's father would ever agree that "muscle is meaningless," but he was able to see the deeper meaning in alternate approaches to earning respect and guiding his son.

Conviction: The Strength That Matters

So, if kindness is perceived as weakness and muscle is meaningless, how is it that we are able to establish our leadership? True leaders do not coerce or cajole, they *inspire* cooperation. The secret to inspiring cooperation lies in authentic confidence, conviction, and compassion. In order for your leadership to be taken seriously, YOU must believe in your own leadership. YOU must be able to experience the strength of your own resolve and the power of your own convictions. Only when you come from a place of centered strength—a place I call "quiet confidence"—can you then be viewed as a worthy leader by either the horse or the adolescent.

Remember that horses and adolescents are looking for worthy leaders, and a worthy leader looks out for the safety and well-being of those in his/her charge. This requires a lot more than simply being nice. And in a given situation, if being nice might put the horse or adolescent in any form of danger, then the worthy leader will be tough. Knowing that the leader can be tough when needed engenders the sense of safety and respect that leads to trust and cooperation.

In the wild, horses live in family groups called herds, which provide an essential sense of safety. In the herd, it is the strongest male that is the lead stallion. It is his job to keep a watchful eye on the safety of the band. If the stallion sends a signal of alarm to the herd, the lead mare (female horse) ensures that the herd moves to safety. In a situation of potential danger, both the stallion and the lead mare will do what is necessary to preserve the safety of the others in the herd. There is no greater kindness than keeping the other horses safe, but to do so, they must often be harsh and demanding, requiring the herd to run and not stop, to climb to higher ground and away from water sources, to move on despite injuries or lack of food. But in so doing, they show themselves deserving of the trust bestowed upon them by the rest of the herd.

In similar ways, we are called upon as trusted adults to move teenagers to higher ground when they are in danger. Often this requires us to be strong and resolute, unwavering and unaffected by their protests. In the end, this is the only way to pass the final test of our leadership and to demonstrate that we are strong enough to ensure their safety in a dangerous situation.

Consider a school fire drill. A fire drill represents a potentially unsafe situation. This is not necessarily the time to be kind and gentle. The important thing in a fire drill is to make sure everyone knows what needs to be done in order to remain safe from the fire. During a fire drill, the administrator in charge must *take* charge. This may mean being firm and demanding. A compassionate leader understands that at this critical time, ensuring safety *is* the kindest thing of all and that doing so may require tough-minded leadership. As Dean of Students, when we held a fire drill, I always prepared for the one or more kids who would act up. I knew that in some primal way, they did so to "test" not only me, but the entire system, to ensure that we could and would provide a safe environment for them.

For parents, there are many times when tough-minded leadership is called for. The young child who wants to stay up late and doesn't realize that they will be exhausted the next day needs a strong parent to deny the request, despite the immediate backlash that is likely to follow. The teenager who wants to go to a party with no supervision and pleads that "everyone else's parents are letting them go," needs a strong parent to recognize the inherent dangers and say no, despite the confrontation that will likely occur. A parent firmly rooted in equal amounts of conviction and compassion can deny the request, offer a brief and honest explanation of the decision, acknowledge the teen's significant disappointment, state with conviction that the decision is based on what is believed to be best for the teen, and withstand the teen's venting of frustration, all with a true expression of compassion. In the long run, this parent will receive more respect than the parent who gives in and lets the teen go to the party.

But the above is a rather tall order, too. Most of us can't pull it off that smoothly. And at times we shouldn't try too hard. Part of the process of becoming an adult is learning to negotiate and compromise. In order for our adolescents to learn this, they need opportunity to practice. At the same time, as adults, we need to recognize that they have more right to contribute to decisions than when they were younger. We have to consider their requests. Doing so is both a sign of respect and a part of reality. Remember that our aim is to elicit cooperation, not mere compliance. Our days of forcing compliance are over. And no amount of mourning the loss of the compliant youngster they once were or yearning for the good old days when we could simply raise our eyebrows in a stern glare and have our children snap into shape will bring back that era. It is gone forever. We must embrace the new age of negotiation and compromise.

The Art of Compromise

Compromise is a valuable skill and one that we should desperately want our budding adults to understand. And while we may effortlessly and effectively use the art of compromise every day, the truth is that we are not used to compromising with teenagers. While we think nothing of the silent negotiation involved in determining whose turn it is at a four-way stop, we feel somehow that we are abdicating our power when we offer a teenager some input into a decision.

Healthy adolescent development is dependent upon our ability to engage in negotiation and compromise with them. I am not exaggerating to say that our survival depends on this. As individual parents or teachers of adolescents, we cannot win a battle of wills. Their drive to be independent is stronger and more primordial than our drive to control. So since they are NOT going to comply without having their say, we may as well let them have it. But there is even more at stake here. As a species, we need to pass on to our emerging adults the ability to negotiate and compromise if we are to progress and flourish. While the importance of this skill cannot be overstated, neither can its need to be taught. The skills of negotiation and compromise are not inherent; they must be learned and practiced.

The underlying forces at play in compromise do not come naturally to most teenagers. Compromise involves several essential factors: a calm discussion among two or more parties, the ability to truly listen to the needs or preferences of the others in the negotiation, and the willingness to forfeit some of what you want in order to have a harmonious outcome.

Most of us do not associate the words "calm," "listening," or "harmonious" with our interactions with adolescents. And likely, neither do they! So this will be new for everyone. As the adult in the mix, we need to set the example. And we may need to be patient while they learn this fine art of compromise. So, start by letting them know that you would like to compromise on a given issue.

Curfew is always a topic that lends itself well to compromise. The parent would like to have the teen in by 8 p.m., and the teen would like to stay out until the break of dawn. Hence, there is *lots of room* for compromise. Tell your adolescent *why* you propose the time that you think is appropriate for curfew. Then, listen while they tell you why it is not a reasonable time. Truly listen. Try to put yourself in their shoes. The more you can really understand their perspective and empathize with what they want, the easier the compromising will be for *them*. Much of the time, the outcome of the discussion is not as important to the adolescent as the experience of being listened to and understood and taken seriously. And remember that, like horses, they smell and detest dishonesty. So, you simply cannot fake this kind of understanding and empathy. You have to truly reach for it inside yourself.

There are two absolutes in listening to your teen at this point. Absolutely *do not* interrupt them. If you do not have enough time to honestly listen to them, ask that the conversation be picked up again later. But do not hurry it. Do not be impatient to get to the compromised solution. Remember that what is most critical here is that the teen knows you are listening and considering his or her point of view. Your teen is learning the art of compromise, and it is a skill that will make your interactions with him or her much easier in the future. It is also a skill that will serve them well for the rest of their life. So, take your time. Model well for them the act of listening respectfully to the view held by another.

The other absolute is that no matter how absurd your teen's point of view may seem, absolutely *do not* laugh (or scoff or roll your eyes). These are not only signs of disrespect and thwart your effort at establishing a more collaborative relationship, but they are also unfair. Your teen is learning a new skill. They have not yet polished the art of articulating what is important to them. Remember, it was not so long ago that when they wanted something, they simply threw a temper tantrum in an effort to persuade you. Persuasion through articulation and discussion is a new skill, and they deserve a chance to practice without feeling self-conscious. Help them if you can. If you understand what they are trying to say and see they are having a hard time putting it into words, try to convey understanding. But *ask* them if your perception is accurate. Allow them to correct you if needed. Remember you are modeling a way of communicating that you probably use effectively at work and in adult relationships. But it may feel very foreign to them.

Once you have truly listened to your teen explain why staying out all night is reasonable, and you have *not* laughed, then you are in a position to reflect back to them what you understood. This is such a critical step and the one most adults ignore. Do not assume that just because you understand your teen's point of view, your teen *knows and believes* that you understand. You must now convince your teen that you have listened and grasped their argument. Doing so does not obligate you to agree with them. It does not suggest that they will get what they want. It simply reassures them that they have been understood.

I cannot possibly emphasize enough the essential nature of this particular point. Unless *they feel truly understood*, the entire conversation is not only meaningless, but it can be counterproductive. They must feel truly understood in order for them to now be open to listening to your response. Invariably, you are not going to fully agree with their position. When you begin to state that you cannot agree to their request, unless they truly feel understood, they will interrupt you with protest. They will state with passion that "you don't understand," that "you never listen to me," "just forget it," or worst of all, the very flippant "whatever" with a dramatic rolling of the eyes. At this point, the conversation is over, and it will be more difficult next time to engage your teen in an attempt at compromise.

Therefore, I must emphasize again the importance of taking the time to ensure not only that you have understood your teen's position, but that *they know* you understand it. I urge you to never skip this step. More than any other piece of advice in this book, I implore you to heed this one. For at this juncture, you are not only working on behalf of your own more harmonious relationship with your adolescent, you are representing adults everywhere. And each of us plays a part in conveying to teens that we are willing to listen and understand them. When any one of us leaves a teen questioning our respect for them and our sincere desire to collaborate, we make it difficult for all the rest of the adults who will come after us. So, consider yourself an ambassador for all adults and tread lightly.

If you have truly listened and successfully conveyed to the teen that you understand their position, then when you begin to explain why you cannot grant their request for a curfew of 4 a.m., they will listen. They might still roll their eyes, but they will generally listen and not interrupt you. You have earned *that much* respect by showing them *that much* respect. If you have not interrupted them and they begin to interrupt you, you can calmly and with validity point out that you did not interrupt them and ask that they show you the same respect. If you can get them to truly listen to your point of view, then the negotiations can begin.

Another important thing to keep in mind during the negotiation phase is that there is no "right" outcome. In fact, the desired outcome is the very process of negotiating itself. There is no formula for arriving at a perfect compromise. You must recall that you are teaching a life skill of the utmost importance. So, the better the teen learns and utilizes the skill, the better their future use of it will be. Realize at the start that if the teen utilizes this new skill with effectiveness, you will likely feel that they have "won" and you have compromised "too much." Both of these are misperceptions. If your teen is using the new skills effectively, *you* have been successful at teaching them. Don't be afraid to let them have a little bit of what they want. Remember that your alternate choice is for them to conclude that your request is ridiculous and defy it entirely. We are aiming for cooperation here, not compliance.

I know many adults might argue that compromising with a teenager is a "slippery slope" and that the teen will try to take advantage of it. I agree. However, I do *not* agree that this is a reason to avoid compromise. Be honest with yourself and recognize that if you have a friend or a boss who easily gives in to your requests, you may try to take advantage of it too. An adolescent's effort to take advantage (I've even heard it described as manipulation) is part of their process of learning how to compromise fairly, how to argue their point, when to give in to others, and how to find that balance point where it feels like a win to both parties. How can they find that balance if you do not negotiate strongly? It is our job to model this process for them.

I also know that in many cultures children are expected to be compliant of adults. When there is an entire cultural system to support this, it works. However, for most teens living in the United States, a fair amount of independence is already granted them. As they move through adolescence, we ask them to assume more responsibility and we grant them more privileges. In our culture, it becomes unproductive and impossible to seek mere compliance from adolescents. Cooperation is a much loftier goal and one that will serve us better in the long run.

I have come to appreciate that compromise is often more than simply finding a middle ground. Sometimes, it is more subtle, as with Mandy. Mandy was an older adolescent, legally an adult, and living independently of her parents. I saw her weekly on an outpatient basis. During one of our sessions that occurred close to an upcoming holiday, Mandy revealed in the final moments that she had recently purchased some "shrooms" and was looking forward to trying them that weekend. Mandy and I had established enough of a relationship that she felt compelled to tell me this relevant information. However, she also knew that I would confront her and make an effort to dissuade her. She didn't want to engage in the dialogue she knew would ensue. By making her disclosure at the end of the session, she could feel that she had both told me this important fact and successfully avoided the discussion about it. The revelation of something significant at the very end of a session is so common that it is referred to among therapists as a "doorknob disclosure."

Knowing that I could not get Mandy to agree in that moment that ingesting psychedelic mushrooms was unwise, I went for the compromise. I asked her if she would be willing to hold off on ingesting the mushrooms until after our next session, to allow us time to talk about the implications and my concerns. Because this was a reasonable request, void of any effort to strip her of her independence or try to control her actions, Mandy agreed. I would have preferred to simply tell Mandy to throw away the dangerous mushrooms, but that was not a realistic option. Likewise, I know a part of Mandy would have liked being told that she could proceed without hearing my concern. However, we arrived at a compromise that we both could tolerate.

I want to take a moment to explain what I meant by "a part of Mandy would have liked..." All of us have some conflicting feelings or goals. However, adolescents seem to live in a constant state of inner conflict. At any given time and in any given situation, there are competing drives within them. In this situation, a part of Mandy wanted to be left alone to get high without having to defend herself or look closely at her motivation. However, another part of Mandy wanted a trusted adult in her life to help her think through the situation and understand her own motivation. She may have even wanted guidance in developing her plan to try the mushrooms. It was this part of Mandy that compelled her to make the disclosure in the first place.

Certainly, Mandy could have left the session without telling me anything about the mushrooms. There are two reasons this is significant. First, in almost any situation, the competing parts of our teenager are present. Knowing which "part" of them we are contending with can leave us better able to engage them effectively. The second reason is that it is extremely useful to reflect to our adolescent that there are these competing parts. By acknowledging that there is a part that would prefer to avoid the confrontation, we honor their choice to make the disclosure and allow the interaction. We also strengthen that healthy part that wants to engage with adults before making big decisions. It is a way of showing respect and appreciation for the relationship that we have developed in which they do see us as a trusted adult.

Horses Are Not Big Dogs

Anyone who has ever tried to train a horse using the same methods they have used successfully with a dog has been sorely disappointed and usually extremely frustrated. Horses are not big dogs! In fact, perhaps the only thing that horses and dogs have in common is that they have been domesticated for several centuries and people throughout time have honored them and incorporated them into their lives in multiple ways. But while dogs are essentially predators who hunt for their food, horses are prey animals, prone to being hunted. As such, they are driven by completely different instincts. Understanding the instinctive fear that drives a horse is essential to training it successfully.

In a similar way, adolescents are not big children, nor are they small adults. To treat them as either one is to make a catastrophic mistake in earning their cooperation. Children accept most of what they are told by an adult with a certain level of faith. They also succumb to the fact that we are older and make the rules. They don't always *like* the rules, but they don't question our ability to set them. Adults, on the other hand, have a level of maturity that allows them to accept certain parameters in society and in the workplace. They seem to almost appreciate that there are rules that contribute to a sense of order and a hierarchy that allows the world to make sense. Hopefully, adults even feel a sense of responsibility to contribute to that sense of order.

Regarding rules and a sense of order, adolescents are significantly different from both children and adults. Teenagers do not accept what we say on faith, and they boldly challenge not only our rules but our very right to set them. They do not embrace the need for order, nor do they accept that there is a natural hierarchy in the world. For an adolescent, *everything* is open to reinterpretation and reexamination, and they easily adopt a new perspective on things that we take for granted. Their world, both internal and external, is entirely different from ours. It is a grave mistake to assume or expect that because they look older than children, they must be thinking more like adults.

As an example, while working with a single mother and her teenage son, in our sessions she repeatedly implored him to explain how he could possibly believe it was okay to act so disrespectfully toward her. She wanted a logical explanation for his behavior. Eventually, I was able to help her see that his behavior was not based on logic—he could not offer her an explanation, and demanding one was essentially a futile endeavor.

She ranted and lectured that he should help around the house and be a respectful member of the family because it was "the right thing to do." I explained to her that for an adult this was logical thinking. Most adults are inherently concerned with what is the right thing to do. However, to her teenage son, there was almost no such thing. There was only what *he wanted* to do. After many sessions, I was able to help her understand that adults want to do the "right thing" because somewhere along the way we learned that it was in our best interest to do so. She needed to ensure that it was in her son's best interest to do what *she* believed was the "right thing." In this way, she could begin to teach him to know right from wrong and eventually instill in him the natural desire to do what is right.

It is not terribly difficult to make it in the best interest of the teen to do something that we want. We simply need to determine what *matters* to them, link the two things, and then return to the 7 C's. *Calmly* and *clearly* explain the association between what they want and what you want. *Confidently* state your expectation. Make clear that they have a *choice* and that each choice carries a *consequence*. Be *consistent* in accepting their choice and enforcing the appropriate consequence. Do so with *compassion*, and eventually your teenager will begin to discover that it is in *his or her* best interest to cooperate with what you want. There will be no more fun or adrenaline in the defiance. There will be no more escaping the consequence with a silver tongue. There will be no more need to argue or grandstand. It will become a matter of routine that there are clear expectations, the allowance to make independent choices, and consistent application of the consequence that has been outlined.

Let's take an example—a universal battle between parents and teens—keeping the bedroom clean. Parents have varying levels of tolerance for the disarray in the typical teen's bedroom. However, even the most relaxed parent wants to feel confident that the room would not be flagged for further investigation if the fire department or Center for Disease Control made a surprise inspection. While the surprise inspection is unlikely, the fact that many adolescent bedrooms would be condemned is not a huge exaggeration. Teens can become extremely territorial, though, and adamantly defend their "right" to keep their room as they see fit. They will staunchly argue that a parent has no right to violate their privacy by going into their room at all, let alone to clean it up or remove dirty socks from the floor. Endless American families have regular battles over this divide.

The answer is really quite simple, and applying it removes significant time on the battlefield. At a calm moment, sit down with your teen and state that it is important to you that their room is kept reasonably clean. Acknowledge that the two of you are unlikely to agree on the standards by which "reasonably clean" is determined. Let them know that your standard is the one that will be used in this case and that you do not expect them to agree with it. Outline exactly what you mean by "reasonably clean" and truly be reasonable about it! Then acknowledge that this will require some effort on the teen's part; therefore, you are willing to reward the effort with something important to them. Either determine together or ahead of time what the important thing is. Important items vary at different times for different teens. Common important items include junk food, new unnecessary clothes, screen time (TV, computer, or video games), time with friends, cell phone usage, money, a ride, or the use of the car. Any of these can be levied against the request for a reasonably clean room.

The critical component is that it become more important to the teen than to the parent that the room gets cleaned and the reward earned. So, for example, a teen who is very clothes conscious wants a new pair of jeans. A parent says, "You want a new pair of jeans, and I want a clean room. So, I will offer to buy you a new pair of jeans after three consecutive weeks of a reasonably clean room. Let me know when you would like to start earning those jeans." Then, the parent leaves it alone, letting the teen decide that this is a good deal (or as good a deal as they are going to get). The parent *lets the teen* initiate the start of the three-week run. For a teen who needs more frequent rewards (i.e., can't wait three weeks for a new pair of jeans), a monetary amount could be assigned to the clean room. If the room is clean on the day it is checked, the teen earns the allowance, which can be set aside or charted so they can see their progress toward earning the new jeans.

The same principle can apply to an older teen who has a part-time job and is earning her own money to buy her own jeans. She wants to use the family car to get to work, because it is much quicker and simpler than public transportation. The parent says, "You want to use the car on a regular basis and I want a reasonably clean room. I am happy to allow you to use the car for any week in which your room remains clean. If it looks messy to me, I will let you know and you can have twenty-four hours to clean it up in order to continue to use the car. If you prefer not to clean your room and take public transportation instead, I can live with that too." Once again, the parent leaves it alone, letting the teen decide whether or not it is worth cleaning the room in order to borrow the car.

It's important for parents to avoid the trap of caring too much about the teen choosing to clean their room. When teenagers feel that we are highly invested in a given outcome, it gives them a sense of power that plays into their drive for independence. Often, they will defy simply to spite us and prove that they are capable of independent defiance. If there is less to defy, cooperation is more likely.

Never Sneak Up On a Horse

Even if you don't know much about horses, you probably know not to sneak up on one. You might even know that you should not walk behind a horse, because they can't see directly behind themselves and it makes them nervous. When horses are nervous, or feel surprised, they can be dangerous. I suggest to you that the same is true of a teenager.

The best way to jeopardize your relationship with a teenager is to sneak up on them or surprise them with something negative. Parents tend to do this when, for example, they let their adolescent get in the car believing they are going one place and *then* announce once the drive is underway that the destination is someplace else entirely—someplace the adolescent does not want to go. I have heard parents justify this to a teen by saying, "I knew if I told you, you wouldn't get in the car."

Teachers make a similar mistake when they call a parent after school hours to report on a student's poor behavior or academic performance. In my opinion (and certainly in the opinion of any adolescent you ask) these are both cheap shots not deserving of respect. And remember, if you don't have respect, you will never get trust, or cooperation.

If you need your teenager to go somewhere, let them know ahead of time with calm and clear confidence that they need to go to this place with you. Acknowledge that they might not want to go. Express ahead of time a level of appreciation that they are going to be cooperative. Give them the benefit of the doubt to be reasonable. Then, if they tell you that they are not going to cooperate, give them some explanation of why it is important that they go. If they begin to protest, simply restate the expectation. When the time comes to depart, they are most likely going to grumble and complain but ultimately will go along with you. Again, express appreciation that they are doing something they don't really want to do.

If the time comes to depart and your teen is truly refusing, then develop your two choices, present them with clear confidence, and let the consequences play out. This could be, "You can come with us and then do what you would like to do later, or you can refuse and expect that I will not be taking you to your friend's house (or the movies or the football game, etc.) later when you want to go." If the teen has another favorite thing, this can be levied against their cooperation. You could say, "I really want you to go, and if you are going to refuse, then I am going to have to disconnect the computer and it will remain disconnected until tomorrow." (Or next week, or whatever seems appropriate *and fair*).

Remember, the key to offering effective choices is that you can truly live with either choice your adolescent makes. Be prepared to take the time to disconnect the computer if that is the choice you offer and the one s/he chooses. And the other key is to NOT lose your cool over it. Express disappointment, even offer an additional incentive if you want, but do not beg and plead or yell and threaten. These only undermine your authority. Remain as detached as possible, and let the consequences unfold naturally.

So, what about the teacher who wants to call a parent about a student's behavior? Unlike therapists who are bound by laws and regulations regarding client confidentiality, teachers and school administrators routinely call home to report problematic behavior or poor school performance. However, doing so without warning conveys a lack of respect and often damages the relationship with the adolescent. In my role as a school administrator, I adhered to a strict rule to never share information without first letting an adolescent know that I would be doing so. If a parent needed to be called, it was my firm policy that the student be told ahead of time and invited to be present when I placed the call.

When I suggested that teachers adopt a similar policy, it seemed to make them very uneasy. As adults, we rarely want to be present when someone is having a discussion about us. But adolescents don't think the way we do. They come from a place of suspicion and fear. By offering to allow them to hear the entire conversation, with the parent on speaker phone, there are no surprises. As a school administrator, I never *asked* the student for permission to call their parent. I *told* them that I needed to call, and then I told them the basic gist of what I planned to report. If there were specifics that I would not disclose, I reassured them that those details would not be included. Then, I simply asked if they would like to be with me when I made the call.

Many teens were initially surprised by this approach. They were not used to adults being quite so upfront and respectful of their need to know what was going on. I capitalized on this by telling them directly that this was a way of showing my respect for them. I told them that I thought they *deserved* to know exactly what was being said about them, and I invited them to correct anything that I unintentionally misrepresented.

Most adolescents accepted the offer to be present when I talked to their parent. When I called the parent, I immediately told them their student was in the room with me and that they were on speaker phone. I reported the given situation as objectively as I could and repeatedly invited the teenager to correct me if needed. I often asked the teenager at the end, "Did I report this situation fairly? Is there any part that you would change or anything that you want to add?" Doing so showed respect and held them accountable, all at the same time. If the account was accurate, they could not deny it in my presence. This also prevented them from going home later and denying it or reporting that I'd lied or misunderstood the situation.

I am a firm advocate of this approach to discussing problems with parents, as it models open communication for the parent, shows respect for the teenager, and eliminates almost any misunderstandings that could occur. Occasionally, I varied this approach and invited the adolescent to go home and report the situation to their parent *themselves*. I let them know that I would follow up the next day to make sure that their parent understood things accurately. I did this to teach the adolescent how to take ownership or responsibility for their own actions. I let them know that most parents would rather hear about a problem directly from their child rather than from a school administrator. For many teens, it was a relief to be able to be the first to "tell their side of the story." However, some teens openly admitted that they probably could not do it and preferred that I call.

It is amazing to me how much compassion and accountability can be conveyed in addressing teens with the same respect that we want others to hold for us. Although no longer a school administrator, I apply a similar approach in my clinical work with adolescents. If I feel something needs to be shared with a parent, I ask the teen how we can best do so together. I explain my reason for wanting to share specific information with their parent and listen to whatever concerns they have about disclosing this information. Most of the time, the teen is apprehensive about their parent's response to the information and I let them know that I will be there to help their parent find an appropriate response. I assure the teen that it is my intention to help their parent understand the situation in a way that allows for them to be more supportive. And I remind them that I need their permission and their help to do so.

By being upfront about my own concerns and listening openly to theirs, I am generally able to negotiate a plan that allows the teen to share delicate information with a parent in a way that enhances family communication and preserves the trust I have established with the teen.

Be Consistently Flexible

There is nothing more certain and consistent than the inconsistency of teens and horses. Mares, in particular, can be very different from one day to the next. And you may not know why one day your horse is able to do something without difficulty and the next he seems completely reluctant. And the truth is it doesn't really matter why. What matters is that you deal effectively with the horse that shows up that day.

The same is true for teens. One day your son or daughter may seem cooperative and pleasant. The next day, for no apparent reason, s/he is belligerent and hostile. One day a student seems engaged in learning and acknowledges your authority, and the next, s/he is disinterested and disrespectful. You can become consumed in trying to figure out why, and sometimes there may be a reason that is helpful to you. However, more often the shift in attitude or behavior is due to factors that will remain a mystery to you. What is essential is that you respect and honor the teen who is before you that day.

This is not to say that you cannot have reasonable expectations. However, it is also reasonable to *expect* that your teen will have mood swings and there will be inconsistency in how they act from one day to the next. Remember that they are dealing with hormonal changes and social pressures that greatly affect the way they feel about themselves and the world around them.

While the reasons are different and the swing is not as dramatic, horses do have moods too. They react with emotion to changes in their environment or the loss of a herd member. They are happier when they receive an optimal balance of work, attention, and rest. To get frustrated, angry, or discouraged is not useful in reacting to either the sullen horse or the moody adolescent. It only serves to drive the adolescent further into their mood. It also reinforces their notion that you are simply one more adult who really doesn't "get it." You can jeopardize the relationship that you have built by expecting it not to shift from time to time. You will seem to lack understanding and expect perfection. Even adults don't like that. And adolescents detest it!

So, your teen is in a bad mood and you don't know why. Their reaction to you is bordering on disrespect. You don't want to escalate the situation, but you also don't want to ignore bad behavior. You feel like you are walking a very fine line. What exactly *can* you do to reinforce the relationship? Acknowledge the bad mood or the distant attitude. Call a spade a spade, but do so without judgment and criticism.

Tell them that you will give them some space and not nag them today. However, you will not accept blatant disrespect.

What the teen needs at this point is the same thing the horse needs: strong leadership based in understanding. This means setting limits on the extent to which the attitude or behavior is displayed, but also accepting the mood or feeling behind it. It *is* a fine line to walk, but it is also possible.

It may help to tap into your own empathy. Imagine that you are not feeling well when you arrive at your job and bump into your boss. You don't expect your boss to let you go home or do nothing on the job, but you also expect a little leeway for the fact that you are not feeling your best. You expect that your boss knows you are usually a strong employee and therefore will give you the benefit of the doubt if you are not performing at your usual caliber. The major differences between you in this situation and the moody adolescent are that they cannot or will not usually explain the source of their shift and their shifts occur more frequently. But the appropriate response is the same. Give a little slack, but don't let them completely off the hook.

Lose the Agenda

In August of 2010, I went to work as an equine therapist for a residential treatment center in southern Virginia. There were twelve horses on the ranch, and I knew that I needed to acquaint myself with each one in order to know how to most effectively incorporate them into our program. I had been given an introduction to each horse and had a sense of their age, breed, training, and general personality. However, horses, just like teens, react differently to different people and different energies. So, I knew that I needed to get to know each one for myself. I set about working individually with each horse to get to know their particular personality and strengths so I could best involve them in our program.

On one particular day, I set out toward the far field where some of our less-utilized horses were grazing. I had determined that I wanted to work with Lily that day. Lily was one of the younger, more spirited horses at the ranch, and she was beautiful. I had taken a fancy to her from the start but also had been warned that she could be rather headstrong and even difficult at times. She had thrown the previous horse trainer, a very accomplished rider, and the other ranch staff were a little wary of her. She intrigued me, and I was excited to begin developing a connection with her.

As I approached her paddock and entered the gate, Lily kept a watchful eye on me. I approached her slowly, with halter in hand, assuming I would be able to halter her easily. However, as soon as I got close enough, she moved slowly but deliberately away. I paused and then approached again, and again she walked away. She could have run far from me or shown signs of aggression, but she did neither. Instead, she repeatedly walked just far enough from me that I could not get a halter on her. I had to make a choice between following my own agenda or respecting her clear wish to be left *un*-haltered.

Now, if you ask most horse people how they think I should have handled this situation, many are likely to say that I should not have "let Lily get away with it" and that by allowing her to avoid the halter that day, I was encouraging "bad behavior" and setting a "dangerous precedent." The truth is that I don't necessarily disagree with them. But I also have learned to respect the horse and trust my intuition. In that moment, my intuition told me I would ultimately get more from Lily if I gave a little. I literally said to Lily out loud, "There will be times when you must cooperate with me, but today is not one of them. I am not sure why you're reluctant, but I'll respect it and trust that on another occasion you will be more willing." I then turned to her herdmate Willy, who seemed almost eager to be haltered, and led him to the arena for some time and attention. I thoroughly enjoyed my time getting to know Willy that day, and when I returned him to the pasture, I half-jokingly said to him, "Hey, do me a favor and tell Lily that it wasn't so bad."

Several days later, I returned to that pasture with halter in hand, curious to see what response I would get from Lily. I knew enough to wonder if I had set a precedent that would be hard to undo. However, my intuition that previous day had been strong. As I approached the paddock, Lily and Willy both watched me from a distance. Then, slowly and deliberately, Lily walked from the back of the paddock toward the gate. As I entered her pasture, she continued to approach. She came close to my chest, lowered her head slightly and stood quietly while I easily haltered her. I led her back to the arena and worked with her for a couple of hours that day. She was willing and engaged; alert and invested. We connected and she became my favorite horse among the many at that ranch.

On subsequent occasions I rode Lily, and she proved to be a very willing horse, sensitive to rein and leg aides, but extremely responsive and cooperative to a gentle rider. My connection with Lily progressed steadily to the point that she would follow me through an obstacle course in a large open arena with no halter or lead rope on—just willing to be with me.

How do I explain my relationship with Lily and what does it have to do with teens? As we have established, any relationship with a horse or an adolescent must be based on respect. Usually, we are so focused on *earning* the respect of the horse or teen through tough-minded and compassionate leadership, that we forget how sometimes *showing* respect is the best way to gain it. I am convinced that for Lily, feeling respected that day laid the groundwork for our relationship. And I think that for many teens the principle is the same. Show some respect and you might get more than you originally imagined in return.

To be fair, that same situation could have gone another way, and I knew it at the time. Many horse people would say that I took a great risk that first day by "letting Lily get away with being stubborn" and that I got lucky, in that she changed her response to me. But what if Lily wasn't being "stubborn"? What if she was in fact testing me to see if I could be a leader who respects those in my charge? What if she wanted to see if I was more invested in my own agenda than in reading her communication?

The truth is that there was *no* reason, other than my own ego or agenda, to dictate whether Lily would *have to* work with me that day. I knew it—and I believe she knew it too. By acknowledging it, I conveyed respect for Lily and accepted her communication that she did not want to be haltered. My decision that day was guided by the important principle of respect. With both horses and adolescents, respect is almost everything, and it has to be authentic. By showing her genuine respect, I gained her respect—and ultimately her trust.

As a principle, this is equally important to remember in dealing with adolescents. Sometimes, it is simply our ego or our agenda that drives us to insist on certain things. We dictate when chores should be done, where students sit in the classroom, what options are available at lunch. Many of these things need to be dictated. Adolescents rely upon us to set the structure and the expectations. However, if we are honest, some of what we dictate is simply driven by what is convenient for us or what fits into our own personal agendas. Sometimes by giving a little, we can get a lot more in return, as I did with Lily that day.

Acknowledge the Try

I am not sure which of the natural horse trainers coined the term first, but I know that I first heard it from Anna Twinney. "Acknowledge the try" is a fundamental principle in her training method and one that makes a lot of sense when applied to both horses and teens. You see, horses sometimes communicate in very subtle ways. To work effectively with horses, one must learn to read these subtle cues correctly and respond effectively. To the untrained eye, a flick of the ear is just that—a horse flicking its ear. But to the sensitive horse lover, a flick of the ear is a significant cue that indicates the horse has shifted from resistance or confusion to trying to understand what is being asked of it. Respond correctly to the flick of the ear and the horse feels understood and encouraged to continue to try and collaborate. Respond incorrectly and the horse feels misunderstood and frustrated, and efforts to connect are thwarted.

I believe this same principle applies to working with adolescents. Too often we miss the subtle, but significant, cues they send. And like the horse, they may not even know they are sending these cues. But if we, as adults, can learn to recognize and respond effectively, we can more quickly improve our relationship with our teen by encouraging them toward continued effort.

So, how do we develop more proficiency at reading the cues that adolescents send? To do so requires a willingness to see the best in our teenagers and to take the time to search for the subtle cues they may be sending. A teen, who has been arguing with his parents all week and has been in trouble at school recently, suddenly makes his bed on Saturday morning. This is what I would call a "try." It is a subtle but recognizable cue that the teen is trying to start the weekend on a different note.

The response to this minor cue can determine the tone of the rest of the weekend. The parent who does not say anything about the bed being made for the first time in ages misses the opportunity to communicate appreciation and encourage continued efforts. The parent who responds with suspicion and concludes that the making of the bed is manipulative in some way actually pushes the teen toward the dangerous conclusion that there is no sense trying and that the relationship cannot be improved. However, the parent who "acknowledges the try" by thanking the adolescent for making the bed, or commenting that it is nice to see, sends the important message that the teen's efforts are recognized and appreciated. This response encourages further effort from the teen.

In the field of special education, the common phrase "catch them being good" conveys this same principle. This phrase reminds teachers and others working with special needs students that it is easy to find their mistakes. But if we only comment on their mistakes, we contribute to the frustration and hopelessness that drive much of their poor behavior. If, on the other hand, we can spot the occasional incident of compassion or self-control from a student who rarely displays it, we can encourage more of the same. By acknowledging the try, we send a very powerful message that we are looking for and believe in their ability to cooperate and to do well. Every teen, whether they have special needs or not, wants to feel that the adults around them are able to see and appreciate the efforts they make toward positive behavior and cooperative interaction.

Take, for example, the student who rarely studies for a test and consistently performs poorly, who then does a little better on a given test. The teacher, who does not acknowledge in any way the improvement made, misses the opportunity to encourage continued studying. Even more troubling is the teacher who somehow makes the student regret the effort by conveying that the improvement this time demonstrates the lack of effort on previous occasions and "proves" that the student has not been trying hard enough. While this may sound cruel, I assure you that the teacher who responds in this manner likely believes they are motivating their student by indicating that they believe the student is capable of better grades than they have been earning. What this teacher fails to understand is that better grades is clearly not motivation enough for this student to study. Acknowledgment, a smile, a pat on the back, a sense of pride, words of encouragement, or positive feedback from the teacher are all ways of "acknowledging the try." These are more likely to inspire continued effort from the student.

Other examples of subtle adolescent "tries" could include:

- Turning in a partially-completed homework assignment when often it is not done at all
- Doing one's assigned chores without being asked
- Turning in an English essay on time, when usually the student is late
- Letting the younger sibling choose the TV channel
- Letting a lower-status kid sit at the lunch table
- Offering less backtalk at bedtime
- Agreeing (even begrudgingly) to help a teacher or an administrator with a task
- Taking medication independently when they have generally needed reminders
- Taking dishes to the sink or dishwasher without being asked
- A slight improvement in the organization of their bedroom or backpack
- More consistent attendance from a student with a history of truancy
- Going to church or synagogue without the typical argument

You may notice that in most of the examples above the effort is only partial or the improvement only slight. You may be tempted to think, "too little, too late." However, I urge you to see it as an opportunity to "acknowledge the try" or the partial success. In doing so, you are encouraging continued effort and even further improvement.

Heed the Warning

Few horses ever kick or bite without first sending multiple warnings. The warnings, or cues, are sometimes subtle to humans. They can include swishing of the tail, an averting of the eyes, a slight turning of the body, or the more easily recognized pinning of the ears. When a horse really pins its ears, the cue is clear and the horse is trying very hard to communicate its irritation and warn of an impending kick or bite. Usually, the pinning of the ears is a final attempt to warn. If we are able to pick up on the more subtle cues, we may be able to avoid pushing the horse to this final and more dramatic cue. I believe the same is true of teens. They send us cues, and when we do not respond effectively they increase the volume or the size of their signal to warn.

All of us have our "breaking point." As adults, we have hopefully learned to manage our frustrations and release our anger in safe and appropriate ways. Adolescents are less proficient at doing this. They are more likely to "fly off the handle" or "explode for no reason." However, usually there are subtle cues that could have predicted their reaction if we were only a little more astute. Reading the warning signs of teenagers requires a willingness to respect that they have their breaking point and to believe that if given some time and space, they will handle a situation better than if they feel rushed and cornered. It means allowing them to influence the timeline instead of insisting on our own. Often, it means recognizing when our pride may be making unrealistic demands. Most adults feel powerless around resistant adolescents and try to regain this sense of power by making demands. This approach almost unilaterally backfires.

The teen who is trying unsuccessfully to gain permission of some kind and continually meets with denial is likely to storm out of the classroom or stomp up the stairs and slam the bedroom door. This is a clear warning that the teen is frustrated. For the teacher to go after the student in anger and insist on more respectful behavior, or for the parent to follow their child upstairs and yell at them for walking away, is as foolish as continuing to irritate a horse when its ears are already pinned. It is ignoring the warning signs and inviting an escalation of behavior. It is a failure to grant time and space for the teen to come around to more reasonable behavior.

I am aware that for many adults it is extremely difficult to let a teen stomp off in anger without addressing the behavior or to ignore the mumbling under the breath that they might do when frustrated. It is hard to heed these warning signs because we somehow feel that we are "letting them get away with it." Granting them time and space is *not* the same as condoning misbehavior. It is simply showing respect for their need to calm down before they are able to engage in reasonable discussion about the issue at hand. It is acknowledging that they can influence the timetable. It is allowing for a teen version of "time out" and having the confidence in our authority to know that we will address the issue later.

Not only is it foolish to pursue an angry teen, it is also ineffective. The adolescent who is caught up in their state of frustration is not able to listen with an open mind, problem-solve, or compromise effectively. If pushed, they will almost always become angrier. It is much like poking a beehive. Instead, I advise that you let them stomp away. Later, when they seem calmer and perhaps are even hoping that you have forgotten their behavior, calmly ask if they are ready to talk about what happened earlier. They may try to feign a look of confusion and deny that they know what you are referring to, but more likely, they will reluctantly but calmly enter into the discussion. I have found that most teens are able to apologize or acknowledge their disrespectful behavior when adults respond with the respect of granting them the time and space to calm down first.

Much like the horse who offers more subtle cues before it pins its ears, most teens have more subtle signs of frustration than stomping away from an adult. I advise that you observe closely and even ask your teen what signs s/he is aware of that might indicate frustration. Look for changes in their breathing, a restless leg or foot, a darting of the eyes or more rapid movement of the eyelids, a clenching of the fists, a cracking of knuckles, a pursing of the lips, a grinding of the teeth, or a rubbing of the thigh. These are among the more subtle indicators that an adolescent's frustration is growing. Often, they are not aware of these somatic cues and helping them become aware can be helpful to them. It is certainly helpful to you as you interact with the teen to know what subtle cues might indicate a growing level of frustration. By intervening early, backing off, changing your tactic, acknowledging their irritation, offering time and space, or simply postponing the conversation, you might be able to avert the mumbling or stomping that comes later.

Pick Your Battles

The concept of "picking your battles" is one of the easiest to understand and one of the hardest to apply. It makes perfect sense that when dealing with imperfect creatures (humans or horses) we need to accept some of the inherent imperfection. We need to acknowledge that things will not always go as we want. We understand that the other has their own agenda and that their agenda may differ from ours. Rarely, have I had to explain to a teacher or parent the notion of "pick your battles." However, I often hear that it is hard to know *which* battles to pick, how many, and at which times. The application of this principle is where most of us need some guidance.

You may not want to hear this, but there are really no hard and fast criteria for applying this important principle. To make matters even more complicated, the application of the principle varies with the circumstances—age, temperament, relationship history, and situational variables all affect the selection of battles. When your child was very young, you certainly picked your battles. If you offered them an apple and they wanted it cut into smaller pieces, you probably obliged most of the time, except when you were driving the car and they simply had to eat it whole. If you told them to put on a sweater and they chose one that wasn't your favorite, you probably let it slide.

When kids are young, it seems easier to determine which things matter and which really don't. As they get older, we become aware that we are teaching them values and helping them establish habits, so we may choose to engage in more battles. Their preference to skip a bath after a soccer or basketball game is met with clear insistence that it is essential for them to bathe. We want them to learn good hygiene habits. However, at some point, they get old enough to make a lot of these decisions on their own. They have been taught the core values and now need to determine for themselves if these are values they will live by.

The important thing is not so much which battles you choose, but that the teen in your life understands the selection. Let's take an example. In a family where participation in a religious institution is a core value and an important part of the parents' lifestyle, attendance with the family may be mandated and may be a battle the parents feel is worth undertaking. In a family where faith is more loosely defined and attendance at a formal religious service is less essential, parents may choose not to require their teen to attend services with them. Neither parent is right or wrong. Both are choosing carefully whether to battle over attendance at religious services. The important thing is that the teen in each family understands that the battle has been determined. In the first family, the teen needs to understand that religious involvement is of paramount importance to the parents and that attendance is mandatory. In the second family, the teen needs to understand that the parents want her to attend services with them, that attendance is important to them, but they are choosing not to force the issue upon the teen.

Letting the teen know you have chosen to battle on a given issue can be a huge advantage if you are a fair and reasonable adult. Most teens will argue but give in to the few things that are mandatory in a family—as long as there are only a few. If there are too many rules and they are all enforced with strict parameters, even the most compliant teen will begin to resent the lack of choice in their life.

Most horses are very sensitive to sound, movement, and touch. Even the lightest pressure on their side will move the trained horse forward, and it should only take a very light touch of the reins to bring the horse to a stop. However, if a horse has been trained with a heavy hand or a rough leg, it can grow accustomed to more dramatic cues from a rider and will seemingly ignore cues that are more delicate. This horse has become desensitized to more gentle touch and therefore recognizes only the more assertive approach.

The same principle applies to children, teens, and even to adults. The boss who is never satisfied and constantly complains about performance will eventually deter employees from trying to please. However, the boss who is easy to please but suddenly conveys disappointment will evoke grave concern from the employees involved. These examples are rather intuitive and may even seem obvious when dealing with adults.

It can be much more difficult, however, to apply this same principle in our interaction with teens. The reason for this is that they tend to "push our buttons." They test us over and over again, trying to see what they can get away with. So, their reactions may not convey that they recognize the compromises we make. I assure you, though, that they do. When you are fair and choose your battles carefully, you can occasionally play your "trump card" and get begrudging compliance from your teen. At this point, I urge you to again choose your battle. Don't *expect* cheerful compliance in this kind of situation. Be content that your teen is acknowledging that you are playing a trump card.

So, let's return to our earlier example of the family who explains to the teen that while church attendance is desired, it is not an issue that the parents are going to *force.* Christmas or Hanukkah approaches and grandparents are coming for a visit. The parents let the teen know *ahead of time* that they will be expected to go to a service with the entire family for this important religious holiday when the grandparents are in town. More than likely, if the parents have chosen carefully, the teen will comply with this request. S/he may grumble or try to tell the parents why it is "not fair." The teen may even say that s/he is not going to do it. But in the end that teen is likely to accompany the family to church at the specified time. The parents in turn would be wise to thank their teen for doing so, acknowledging that they understand s/he didn't want to come and that s/he is doing it out of respect for the parents and grandparents.

The Energy Equation

Over the years, I have continued to learn about horses and adolescents and have continued to see their similarities. My knowledge of horses has always informed my approach with adolescents, and occasionally something I knew to be true of teens proved to be useful in my approach with horses. For instance, I was in Colorado for a workshop during one of the worst forest fires in Colorado's history. As the fire raged in the hills nearby, we were poised and ready to evacuate the horses and ourselves. I was sent to the barn to put halters on each of the horses so moving them could be done more swiftly and efficiently when the time came. As I headed out the door, I was reminded to "check my energy." I took a deep breath and headed out to the barn.

Over the years, I have developed a deep appreciation for how horses respond to human energy. When we are anxious or upset, the horse literally feels our heightened energy and reacts to it. Usually, they feel confused and agitated. They sense that we are anxious and conclude there must be danger nearby. On a primal level, they conclude that if the predator in their midst is nervous, things must be really bad. This concept fits perfectly with what I know of adolescents and reaffirmed a principle I had been teaching for years.

In a crisis situation with a teenager, it is essential to be aware of and in control of your own energy. When a teenager is upset and yelling and cursing, our instinct as adults is to set the limits and regain control of the situation. Most of us tend to do this by either yelling louder or threatening a consequence of some kind. Although our intent is to regain control of the situation, we usually exacerbate it. Often, our own energy combines with the energy of the angry adolescent and leads to a heightened intensity that begins to feel completely out of control.

When an adolescent is upset or angry, they bring forth a powerful amount of energy. Unfortunately, adults tend to respond with a similar amount of intensity. Usually the result is a significant escalation of both volume and emotion until both parties are engaged in a screaming match or worse. I'm sure you have seen or even participated in this scenario. Typically, it begins with a teen making a snide comment under his breath. The parent replies with a sharp, reprimanding tone, saying something like, "What did you just say?" The teen then restates the snide comment more clearly, with a tone of challenge in his voice. At this point, the parent feels their authority is under attack and raises their voice to try to exert influence or control. The teen feels that his very autonomy is being challenged and responds with an equal amount of indignation and intensity. The dialogue continues back and forth, with steadily increasing volume and intensity. Ultimately, this scenario ends in one of two ways. Either the argument escalates to a physical confrontation or one party backs down. In either case, everyone loses.

It is clear to see how a physical confrontation is a loss for both sides, but what about the scenario in which the teen backs down? Why is that a loss? Remember that the teenager's job is to try to assert independence and to learn to do so with increasing finesse. Backing down only serves to further frustrate the teen, maybe even to the point that next time they will stand their ground until a physical altercation breaks out. They have not learned how to calm themselves and express themselves effectively. And the adult has missed an opportunity to model this for the teen. Instead, both have simply displayed loud and aggressive behavior.

In the early years of my career, I learned an extremely effective technique for deescalating situations like the one described above. The principle behind the technique is quite straightforward, but somehow seems counter to our instincts as adults in positions of authority. It simply says that when the energy in a situation increases beyond an optimal level, lower your *own* energy to bring the situation into balance and ultimately back into control. The irony is that by *lowering* your own energy, you take back control of the situation. Initially, it feels as though you are allowing the angry adolescent to outshout you. However, as the adolescent's volume and tone begin to shift in response to yours, it is clear who is driving the interaction.

Allow me to provide an example. Your teenage son is agitated and begins to yell and curse. You may *want* to yell back, but instead, you lower your voice and very calmly and firmly state that his yelling is unacceptable. You ask him very calmly and firmly to stop yelling so that the two of you may discuss the situation. At first, he continues to talk to you in a disrespectful manner and a loud tone. You calmly and firmly restate your request that he lower his voice and gain control so that the two of you can discuss the situation. While he tries to engage you in his angry discourse, you resist the draw. As long as he is yelling and cursing, you do *not* respond to anything he says. He cannot get a reaction from you other than your request that he calm down and lower his voice. Eventually, even the most highly agitated teen will calm down.

For those who have entered a rare state of true rage, the timeframe for calming down will be longer. Regardless of the timeframe, in the presence of *only* their own energy, most teens will return to a state of homeostasis, or balance. By *not* playing into their demands for a battle, you have exerted the higher influence on the situation and subtly reestablished your authority in the process.

Trust is the Goal

We have spent the better part of this book talking about how to earn an adolescent or horse's respect. However, the ultimate goal is to earn their trust. In all earnestness, and with over twenty-five years of experience, I submit to you that once you have truly earned their respect, you will have earned their trust. And with their trust comes a certain degree of reliable cooperation from both horses and teens.

Recall that for herds of wild horses throughout time, their mere survival depended upon trusting the herd stallion and the lead mare to preserve their safety. Once the stallion or lead mare earns the respect of the others, they also earn their trust. And both the stallion and lead mare take seriously their place in the herd and preserve their leadership by remaining deserving of the trust.

In a similar way, we too must be careful to preserve the trust we have earned from the adolescents in our life. Although it must be painstakingly won, it can be easily destroyed. Divulging things told to us in confidence, snooping around their room or reading their emails without them knowing, assuming information given by others is true without letting them explain their own point of view, overlooking something that is important to them, or even a simple overreaction on our part can undermine the trust that took so long to earn.

Being so hard to earn and so easy to lose, it is natural to wonder if having their trust is even worth all the effort. If you have ever had an adolescent's true trust, you know that it is. They are the future generation, facing the task of determining their values and their own character. They will one day be developing policy and enforcing laws. In order to have any influence in how they turn out and how they ultimately steer our society, we must have their trust. If we do not have it, others will. Perhaps a neighborhood gang, a misguided adult, a cult, or even worse, perhaps they will conclude that they can trust no one. They might never learn what it means to trust and to be deserving of trust. They will not be able to pass a sense of the importance of trust on to the generation after theirs.

Trust is our only means of truly and positively influencing the individual adolescents in our lives and the collective of their generation. Without it, we are simply lumped together with all the adults who are unworthy of respect and trust. We are dismissed and ignored, patronized and pacified with insincere platitudes, lies, and façades. Without it, we are on the outside watching helplessly as they navigate a complicated and dangerous world on their own. Without it, we are not privy to their struggles and their victories; we do not have the relationship that allows us to be an integral part of their lives. Without it, we lose out altogether on any meaningful connection to them and to the next generation. So, make no mistake about it—their trust is a precious and precarious prize that is worth every test we endure to earn it and worth taking all measures to protect.

Learning Along with Them

One of the greatest joys of working with both adolescents and horses is the immense amount that you learn about yourself in the process. Horses and teens will teach you about patience, energy, your own biases and convictions. Through interactions with them you will further define your values and examine your core beliefs. Both will challenge you to be a better person. You will want to rise to the occasion, to meet the challenge of earning their trust and cooperation. You will develop skills of self-awareness and self-control that you didn't have before and will be both humbled and honored in the process.

Sharing with an adolescent what you have learned from them can be a tremendous gift. Despite their bravado, most teens feel somewhat insignificant and are surprised to learn that they have helped an adult to grow. By letting them know what you have learned from them, you offer two things. First, you model that learning and growing are lifelong ventures and that you are never too old to improve your personal effectiveness. Second, you challenge them to begin to see themselves as affecting others and influencing those around them, and to recognize their inherent value and strengths.

By focusing on their positive qualities, we help those qualities to grow. Since teens are in such a state of change and exploration, there are usually many aspects to them that we can highlight. Highlight those that are most positive, instead of the ones we wish would diminish. In doing so, we help our teens to see those positive qualities more clearly, and as a result, those positive qualities will grow and develop.

Paint the Picture You Want to See

Sometimes by reflecting back to a teen those qualities that we see in them, we can help them see it in themselves. Even if there is only an occasional glimmer of that positive quality, it is still worth mentioning. In fact, perhaps it is those attributes only revealed on occasion that are *most* worth mentioning, for it is these qualities that they are unlikely to see in themselves.

The example of Antonio comes to mind. Antonio was a tough teen and a bit of a loner at school. He had a reading disability but was otherwise more savvy and mature than many of our students. About 50 percent of our students had social difficulties and often made social blunders that rendered them vulnerable to teasing. The rest of our student body had learning disabilities but were quite current and effective socially. When one of the kids with social difficulties made a blunder, it was generally one of these "cooler" kids who teased them or made fun of the situation. This is not uncommon among teens, and a large part of my job was navigating the needs of these two distinct populations and helping them to appreciate one another. The kids with social difficulties could learn a lot from those with more socially appropriate behaviors, and the kids with learning difficulties could learn a lot academically from the others.

Antonio was among the cooler kids, and many of our socially challenged students were intimidated by him. He had a tough exterior and a reputation for fighting. He was a "top dog" in our school. Yet, I noticed that he was never involved in the teasing. On one occasion, I heard him defend a kid who had made a social blunder by simply telling another kid to "back off" when he began to tease him. Antonio's statement was short and his tone was not hostile. But he had a presence about him that inspired others to take him seriously. The other kid ceased his teasing. Unfortunately, the kid who had made the blunder was not socially astute enough to even notice the way Antonio had intervened on his behalf, so he made no effort to express appreciation.

Later that day, I asked to see Antonio in private and I shared my observations. I attempted to "paint the picture" I wanted Antonio to see. I told him that I saw him as a "champion of the underdog" and that I respected the way he used his strong and demanding presence for the benefit of those who had less of a presence and were more vulnerable to teasing. I told him that I saw in him a real kindness and sensitivity toward others that he only revealed on occasion. I told him that I knew he had the presence and popularity to show kindness without jeopardizing his status or reputation among others. I encouraged him to use this wonderful ability more frequently.

Antonio was a quiet kid. He made little reply to what I said. He looked at me a little quizzically and sort of shrugged. I wondered how much he was taking in, but I knew enough to understand that in Antonio's life he had not often been asked to see a school administrator in order to receive a compliment. Most likely, he'd never heard anyone reflect on his positive character.

Over the next few months, I watched as Antonio more openly defended other kids in our school. At one point, he took on one of the more active "bullies" in his typical brief and effective style. He simply said, "You need to find something else to do. And I mean it." It gradually became known that teasing would not be tolerated by Antonio, and as a result, the teasing in our school was minimal that year. More than just diminishing the teasing in our school, Antonio actively developed his own identity as a defender of those weaker than he. I presented a picture for Antonio, and he chose to continue to develop it. Sometimes, I wonder how many other kids could have been helped if I'd taken more time to show them the qualities that lay dormant or latent in them and then encouraged them to see those qualities and develop them within themselves.

Kindred Spirits

As we have been exploring the similarities between horses and teens, you may have identified with a few of the qualities yourself. Most of us (perhaps all of us) harbor an "inner adolescent." As adults, we still *feel* rebellious at times and occasionally want to challenge the status quo or forge a new trail. However, temperament and circumstance determine how much of our wildness we express in our daily lives. We may even find that we envy those who more readily express wildness the way teens do.

Adolescents and horses live with fervor, sometimes even with complete abandon, being fully in the present moment and often failing to anticipate the consequences of their actions. They are wild at heart and resist those who try to tame them. They are true to themselves, in the immediate moment, and when the moment shifts, so too might their expression of self. They live with bravery and spontaneity, and they inspire and challenge us to do the same. They demonstrate a boldness that we find both compelling and intimidating, yet strangely familiar. We are reminded of the brashness we once possessed ourselves, and we begin to recognize that we are, indeed, *kindred spirits*. By tapping into that part of ourselves, we are better able to understand and appreciate both horses and adolescents.

Be honest with yourself for a moment and reflect on the things you do when you feel a little rebellious. Surely, there are things that you "know you're not *supposed* to do" but do anyway. Think about the times when you say, "Hell with it!" and do something despite your better judgment. Perhaps you drive slightly over the speed limit, knowing the chances of being pulled over are minimal and *worth the risk*. Do you ever go to a fast food restaurant and order something that you *know* you will regret eating but decide in that moment that you *just don't care about the consequences?* Most of us have made an irresponsible purchase at some time or another, wanting something that we knew we really didn't need and definitely couldn't afford. We went ahead anyway, by putting it on credit, deciding we'd "*figure it out later*."

Think about the times when you have allowed yourself to let go and let loose. For instance, have you ever found yourself turning up the radio to a favorite old song and driving with your music blaring, like you did when you were younger? Maybe you went so far as to sing along at the top of your lungs. Have you ever *enjoyed the rush* of telling someone off...or caught yourself flipping someone the bird in traffic? Ever contemplated buying a motorcycle or a jet ski for the sheer thrill it would provide? Would the people who work with you Monday through Friday be surprised to see how you dress or what hobbies you engage in on the weekend? Are you among the many adults who seek vacations that include adventure—white water rafting trips, treks deep into the rainforest, or African safaris?

Most of us can relate to at least one of the above examples (or think of something similar). And in so doing, we can begin to recognize our own wild spirit and bold nature. That boldness is a quality inherent within all of us. It is a part of the very fabric of American culture. Pictures of wild mustangs running free on the open range capture for many the essence of freedom and the American dream. It is this quality of wildness that links horses and adolescents in spirit. And it is a quality that resides within each of us, even if rarely expressed.

Sadly, the wild mustang is currently endangered in the U.S.[1] The United States Bureau of Land Management routinely rounds up wild horses and corrals them into small pens under the premise that these horses are interfering with farming and other land uses. The unnecessary cruelty in this atrocious practice is hidden from most Americans. And almost invariably, those who become aware of it are deeply disturbed. The deep sorrow we feel when we see wild mustangs in captivity, separated from their herds and natural way of life, stems largely from mere compassion. However, the *intense* anger and grief it stirs within us also suggests our connection with these wild animals and our own wild nature. On some level, we sense that we are in danger of losing this national symbol

1. For more info on wild mustangs, go to http://www.themustangproject.org.

of freedom, just as we have lost much of our own bold nature in the process of becoming a responsible adult.

However, we truly need not lose either one. We can tap into our own adolescent spirit of rebellion and harness it to fight the establishment that is trying to extinguish wild mustangs and tarnish our symbol of freedom. Even if we choose not to take up this worthy cause, we can find other causes or occasions when our courageous spirit can be put into action for good. Although time and responsibility may have tempered our boldness, it still lurks within. It can inspire us to take a calculated business risk, speak our truth uncensored, or take a stand for what we believe in. Every time we do so, we nurture our "inner adolescent," and we honor the wild horses and the adolescents in our lives that keep us in touch with that bold part of ourselves. They remind us that we are *all* a little ***Wild at Heart.***

I challenge you to take this a step further and find an old photograph of yourself as a teen. It can be a photo from high school, college, or even early adulthood. Look at it and reflect on that time in your life. See if you can recall the sense of endless possibility that you felt. See if you can recapture the strength and courage that stemmed from feeling invincible. Remind yourself of some of the senseless risks you took and the way you likely relished the adventure. See again the horizon before you and know that you are not as limited as you may have come to believe. Deep within you, ready and wanting to be accessed, is a spirited, wild, brave heart that will lead you boldly in a new direction or take you further down the path you are currently on, if only you will allow it.

Try to honor your own wild heart and see yourself as a

kindred spirit with both horses and teens. Allow this to guide you in connecting with the teens in your life. Perhaps it will inspire you to become a voice for the wild mustang, an advocate for youth, or a force for change in some other needed area. At the very least, it will allow you to remain, yourself, ***Wild at Heart***.

PART II

Where the Two Creatures Diverge

Finding Themselves

As much as adolescents and horses have in common, there are also some essential differences. Horses know exactly who they are. They live in the present moment and do not worry about what lies ahead or suffer emotional angst over what has occurred in their past. As humans, we are both blessed and cursed with a brain that thinks in reverse and fast forward. We carry pain and anger from the past and we worry about the future. Adolescents are no different. Additionally, given the primal importance of their peer group affiliations and the conflicted relationship they have with family, they spend a lot of time "fretting" about things. All this "fretting" is a necessary part of their process to figure out who they are.

Many teens go through a lot of trial and error in their quest to find themselves. They literally experiment with lifestyles the way any of us try on clothes to find the outfit that best fits and suits us. It is not unusual for an adolescent to spend a few months or a year enjoying sports and spending time with other athletes, playing the part of a "jock," and then return to school after a holiday break dressed in "punk" or "grunge" attire, trying out the role of a "skater" or a "gangster." It is a mistake to get too involved in this process. As adults, the best thing we can do is acknowledge the shift in appearance and continue to treat the teen in the same manner we did before. Deep down, under the baggy pants or the purple hair is the same hurting, searching kid that we have known all along. It is also helpful to talk to them about what they like or don't like about the style or lifestyle they are now drawn to. This acknowledges that they have reason to be interested and shows your interest in them. It also helps them formulate and articulate their own values.

It is important not to get hung up on any of the styles that you don't personally like. This process of theirs is not a personal affront to you. It is not an attempt to embarrass you in front of your friends or neighbors. It is simply their self-exploration. Stand back from it and see it as such. Appreciate the task they are taking on, the task of discovering who they will be in the adult world. Too many parents become concerned about the outer appearance and lose sight of the bigger issue of personal development. Criticizing or fighting your teen on what is essentially a stylistic preference is taking on a losing battle. The hard truth is that they will one day be able to dress and live as they want. Your illusion of control over this area is just that, an illusion. Focus on the real issues of respect and responsibility, good judgment and good character.

When I worked in an intensive outpatient recovery program, there was a young man who arrived at our group sessions with a different hair color and style each week. His dress was fairly consistent with the "punk" style of attire, but his hair was drastically different every week. His parents were both rather clean-cut and conservative. They were both professionals respected in their own domains. They could easily have focused on their son's dramatic and shifting appearance. However, they knew better. They focused exclusively on their son's recovery efforts and school achievement. I ran into them at a conference many years later and asked about their son. I learned that he was still clean and sober and working a recovery program. At the time, he was living in New York, working for a prestigious hair salon. And, of course, his specialty was hair color!

Unfortunately, we are not all as farsighted as this young man's parents were. So, how exactly do you look beyond what can be a very distracting or even disturbing appearance? For some, it helps to draw upon a time in your own life when you experimented or underwent a change. It may be as simple as changing your major in college or moving to a new neighborhood or part of the country that felt more like home to you. Many of us have changed careers.

These personal changes are useful in helping us tap into that part of ourselves that understands the need to try things on for size before we know if they really fit. So, try looking at the baggy, sagging pants of your teenager or her overdone makeup and recall a time when you were different from how you are now. Take a deep breath and take comfort in knowing that teens are in process. As they grow and mature, most teens do not continue to express themselves as dramatically. Look into their eyes; engage their minds; reach out to their hearts. Try to get to the real person underneath the clothes and makeup. When you do, you will also be helping them to find that person too.

Self-Reflection

Horses are not really capable of self-reflection. They accept their own condition and present themselves with pure authenticity. They have little to reflect on. Adolescents, however, are very capable of self-reflection and spend a lot of time engaged in this process. To some adults, it may seem that they are self-absorbed. Remember that part of their self-absorption is developmental and appropriate. They are finding themselves, and it takes some focus on self to do so. Their natural propensity for self-reflection can be a powerful tool for parents or teachers.

The secret to using this tool effectively is to recognize the inherent value in the *process* of reflecting. It is critical for you to recognize that much of what they *say* may be part of their experiment. They may be trying it on for size to see if it fits. Do not allow yourself to become invested in *what* they say, simply aim to engage them in thought-provoking discussions. You are giving them a big gift by probing their thoughts and stimulating their perspective. Be honest with them. If you disagree with their opinion, listen to what they have to say. Tell them what you think. Do *not* try to change their mind. Do *not* aim for agreement. Aim merely for the discussion. They may be arguing with what you say, but all the while they are also taking it in.

Do not be surprised if a few weeks later you overhear that same teen espousing your view or opinion with conviction as though it were his long-held belief. And if you do overhear such a discussion, resist the temptation to make a snide comment or point out that you told him that a week ago. Let him have ownership of his newly-found perspective and take quiet joy in knowing that you influenced a young mind.

At the end of this book is a list of resources to help stimulate discussion with teens. There are many such products on the market, and I have used a variety of these through the years in facilitating teen groups. I have provided you with my favorite tools for enticing teens to talk.

Over the years, I have found that the answers given during a discussion may be merely a temporary trial of the person's thinking on a particular issue. It is really a valuable endeavor to get a teen thinking with you on a topic worthy of discussion. Be prepared for the verbal discourse and detach entirely from the notion of getting the teen to agree with you. What they say in that discussion may have little relevance to their true beliefs or to the beliefs they will adopt more permanently. They may be engaging you to see how you back up your claim. Some adults continue to engage in this type of discourse. We call it "playing devil's advocate" or "for the sake of debate." Teens simply do this naturally.

Taking Responsibility

One of the most significant differences between horses and adolescents is that adolescents can be asked to take verbal responsibility for their behavior. The behavior of a horse is driven largely by instinct and learning. They respond to the moment and engage with humans in a truly authentic manner. They don't plan ahead or strategize. They don't succumb to peer pressure. They don't have weighty decisions to make or the need to exercise good judgment. While they certainly make choices and can learn to think things through, it is not in their nature to manipulate or deceive.

Adolescents, on the other hand, are capable of strategizing and applying good judgment. They are also vulnerable to peer pressure and prone to manipulation. Learning to take responsibility for their choices in life is a critical developmental task. To support them in this task, I highly recommend having adolescents involved in setting up the rules and determining consequences for both positive and negative behavior.

When I counsel parents or teachers on this, I find that many adults seem to feel that they are *relinquishing* their own power by giving an adolescent some decision-making power regarding the rules at home or in the classroom. In fact, the opposite is true. The very fact that they need your invitation to participate reinforces your position of authority and demonstrates that you are a fair and considerate person of authority. By offering to allow the adolescent to participate in the decision-making, you are essentially reinforcing that it is ultimately your authority to delegate.

Most adolescents are actually very fair-minded and will participate in establishing rules in a more mature manner than one might expect. Their mere participation is a victory on many levels. First, in engaging in the *process* of setting up rules, the teen acknowledges that there must *be* rules. When they help to determine what the rules are, they feel a greater level of investment in following the rules and are less likely to defy them. The process itself also teaches them to think in a fair-minded way and to acknowledge the reason behind the rules and the natural consequences of breaking them. However, the *real* victory is that we eliminate some of the conflict when a rule *is* broken. And be assured, even though they help develop the rules, they *will* still break them. Remember their job is to test us, and they will test us to see what we will do when they break the rules, even if they set the rules themselves. However, when they have helped to establish the rules *and* the natural consequences for breaking them, then you can enforce the consequence with very little argument or protest from the teen. If they do protest, simply say, clearly and with compassion, that they *knew* the consequence ahead of time and chose it themselves.

In my tenure as a Dean of Students, I often allowed students to choose their own consequence. I did so once they knew me and our program well enough to know what a typical consequence for their behavior might be. I was repeatedly impressed with how accurate and even severe their self-chosen consequences were. This was a clear indication that the teen had internalized the principle behind the rule and felt some level of regret for their behavior.

Often the *only* thing that can curb a behavior pattern involving more than one student in a school or child in the home is to give them the responsibility of establishing the boundaries. As Dean of Students, I struggled for a couple of years to contend with the amount of "horseplay" that some of the boys engaged in with one another. Despite rules against horseplay or rough housing or physical contact of any kind, they repeatedly shoved each other playfully and tried to trip one another in the hallways. Part of the game was to do so when teachers or other staff were not looking. Then, someone would get caught and suffer a consequence and feel personally targeted since "everyone else does it too."

My personal policy at the time was to investigate *every* behavior write-up in order to allow the students to tell their side of the situation and to help them develop the ability to take responsibility for their behavior. I found myself irritated by the repeated discussion about horseplay. The majority of the teachers saw it as aggressive behavior and the kids unilaterally insisted that it was just in fun. I had little effect those first two years in curbing the behavior.

The following school year, the issue of horseplay among the students seemed worse than ever. This time, instead of starting into my usual procedure, I did something drastically different. I established a "Horseplay Task Force" and called a lunchtime meeting of all the key players in the horseplay. I acknowledged that the adults in the school might misperceive the intent of their behavior. I explained that other students who were not a part of their play might also misinterpret their behavior and even feel uncomfortable or threatened by what looked aggressive to them. I admitted that I personally believed it was in play and not hostile. Then, I reinforced that I also felt it was an important rule in our school and would remain a rule.

I gave them an analogy most of them could easily relate to. "As far as I see it, horseplay in school is a lot like speeding on the highway. I might think that the speed limit is too low. I might know that I can safely drive faster than the posted speed. And I might speed along and not get caught. However, when I do eventually get pulled over, my own opinion of the speed limit is really not up for discussion. The cop does not discuss with me why it is an important law to follow. He or she simply gives me a ticket and I pay it. And I tend not to grumble about how unfair it is because I knew the speed limit and chose to take my chances. So…from now on I am not going to pull you out of class to discuss with you your violation of a rule that you know perfectly well. I am going to treat horseplay like a traffic violation. And you are going to determine the 'cost' of the ticket. I am going to give you the rest of this lunch period to talk amongst yourselves about this.

"Ms. Jones will be in here for supervision only. She is not going to assist you in the discussion or help you determine the consequence. This is up to you. If you deliver to me a proposed consequence that is reasonable, I will agree to it and we will go forward with that as the consequence for future violations. All violations up to now are absolved by your participation in this "Horseplay Task Force." If, however, you deliver to me a proposed consequence that is not reasonable, your task force will meet again tomorrow at lunch...and every day after that until we have an agreed upon consequence. So, I urge you to be serious about this and to talk openly about what it will take to really minimize the horseplay."

With that, I left the room. Since lunch period was short, the group did not have enough time to agree upon a consequence by the end of lunch that day. And I suspect that conversation and negotiations went on after lunch and possibly even after school that day, because only ten minutes into their lunch meeting the next day, the group had agreed to a consequence and asked me to join them for their proposal. I was shocked at what they had come up with.

In our point system, in which privileges were earned by points, they had imposed a loss of points higher than *any* other violation in the school program. Their proposal meant that horseplay would "cost" more than physical aggression. They had always resented the misperceived assessment that their horseplay *was* aggressive, so I questioned why such a steep consequence. The answer I got was one I will always remember. "The only way for us to really stop is to make it high stakes. Anything less is not going to really matter enough to stop the fun."

With that, I acknowledged their honesty and their maturity and thanked them. From that point on, horseplay violations cost the amount of points proposed by the task force and horseplay diminished dramatically. I *think* my students learned a valuable lesson in the process, but I *know* that I did. I learned not to underestimate the value of input from your key players, even if they are mischievous adolescents.

So, what might this look like at home? Let's assume that your teenager is repeatedly coming in late from curfew. You sit up waiting and worrying and when they finally stroll in the door, they act like you are overreacting. I suggest that you sit them down in a calm moment (remember the 7 C's). Ask them if they understand *why* it is important that they stick to their curfew. Have them list as many reasons as they can (for them to get enough sleep, safety, for you to get enough sleep, for them to learn to stick to their agreements, etc.). Then ask them what they think is a reasonable curfew.

Likely, there will need to be some discussion here. Remain open to their input, but also express your concerns. Once you have agreed on a reasonable curfew, then ask them what they think is a reasonable consequence for coming in late. They may try to skirt the task by telling you "I don't know" or "that's up to you." Do *not* let them get out of it that easily. If they agree to a consequence, they are less likely to violate their curfew. You can make some suggestions (grounded for a period of time, earlier curfew the next time, extra chores, loss of the car, TV, etc.). But it is very important that whatever the consequence is, your *teen* has not only agreed to it, but has been critical and active in developing it. Then, the next time this teen breaks curfew, you can simply remind him or her that they knew the rule and the consequence. Generally, this eliminates a great deal of the friction caused when teens are given consequences.

Saving Face

Horses generally do not get embarrassed. They live too much in the moment to give thought to how other horses will perceive them. On the contrary, teens give an immense amount of thought and place a high level of importance on how they are perceived, especially by other teens. For this reason, the concept of allowing them to "save face" among their peers can be critical in eliciting cooperation. In fact, a peaceful resolution to many situations can revolve around the adolescent's ability to "save face."

A parent who wants to address an issue with a teen is wise to ask to speak to the teen *alone,* outside the earshot of the teen's friends—even outside the view of those friends. Alone, the teen may be inclined to listen, especially if you have established yourself as a compassionate parent who demands respect. However, in front of friends, even the most docile teen will not want to look like he is afraid of or controlled by his parents. He may display uncharacteristic defiance simply to impress his peers and establish his credibility among them.

Similarly, a teacher having difficulty with a teen in class is wise to ask to speak to that student *outside* of the classroom. If possible, ask to speak to the student at an entirely different point in time when any defensiveness might be minimized and the teen can listen more openly. Try to establish a positive relationship with the teen. It can also be effective to elicit the teen's cooperation by assigning them a positive role to play in the classroom, or in the school.

As Dean of Students, I regularly held school meetings or assemblies to discuss important events, to reinforce rules or policies, or to generate school pride. On occasion, I became aware of a student who was causing difficulties in several classes and seemed to be striving for attention from peers and staff. As a proactive measure, I would speak to the student prior to the school meeting and ask for their help in some aspect of the meeting. Sometimes my request was as simple as asking that they help a student in a wheelchair to get settled in the assembly. At other times, it was as involved as asking them to be the scribe to help me keep track of the student input on a given issue we planned to address that day. Regardless, the invitation to be a part of the meeting invariably provided a means for the student to earn attention without disruption.

When a student is a part of something, they are far less likely to disrupt it. They are able to "save face" among their peers by standing out in a more positive way. A student prone to disruptive behavior is rarely solicited for leadership tasks and feels truly honored to be chosen. They invariably take the assignment quite seriously. By having them play a role in the meeting, you elicit their cooperation and support ahead of time and divert the potential for their disruptive behavior. I have seen many teachers use this same approach effectively by having a struggling student be their "helper" in some fashion in the class.

Another way to allow a teen to "save face" is to offer an *alternate* authority figure. Many times as Dean of Students, a teacher would request that I come to the classroom to assist with a defiant student. It was quite typical that although the student had refused to leave the classroom upon the teacher's request, he would comply almost as soon as I arrived at the door.

Unfortunately, some teachers mistakenly assume this is a negative reflection on their lack of influence over the class. Even more unfortunate is that some school administrators make the same erroneous assumption. Both fail to recognize that the true agent of change is the power of alternate authority that allowed the adolescent to comply and "save face" among his peers. Once they have defied a teacher publically, the average teen feels they cannot back down. They will hold their ground at all costs in order to appear worthy in the eyes of their classmates. However, when a new authority figure enters, it somehow resets that stage and the teen is able to comply without embarrassment.

Where teachers work with co-teachers or aides, this is a valuable concept to master. Have the aide give a student some direction. If the student fails to comply, wait a bit and then have the teacher make the same request. You will be amazed at how often this small measure is effective. Where parents are fortunate to be co-parenting, the same principle can be applied. If a child defies one parent, allow the other parent to try to elicit cooperation. As long as the roles are constantly shared, there is no risk of undermining one parent's authority. I do warn, however, against the proverbial "wait until your father gets home…" as this sets up a perception that mom is not the "real" authority figure. But do not ever be afraid to share the role of eliciting cooperation. By allowing the teen to respond to someone different, you offer an opportunity for him to safely dig himself out of the hole he has placed himself in with the other party.

Often, we do not have a co-parent or a co-teacher available, so another way to allow a teen to comply while saving face is to allow his compliance to go "unseen" by you. If you have given a directive and stand watching for the teen to obey, you are putting him or her under undue scrutiny. It's best to simply give the directive and then turn away. Trust (or hope) that the teen will comply. Check in after a minute to see if s/he has. If not, go back and restate calmly the directive. The teen may be simply testing to see if you will forget or "let it slide." Return and reiterate your request, but again, allow the teen to comply without your watchful eye upon them. When they do comply, do not make a big deal about it. They may be hoping their peers didn't notice that they complied. Later, in private, you might want to acknowledge their cooperation, but allow them to "save face" in the moment.

It's Not Fair!

Horses are not concerned with fairness the way adolescents are. They do not measure the amount of hay given to another horse and determine that they are being treated unfairly. However, anyone who spends any amount of time with teenagers is likely to hear the common protest that "it's not fair!" It is natural for teens to be aware of what appears to be injustice around them. The truth is that their very lot in life is not really fair. They are expected to be responsible young adults, but they do not enjoy the rights that go with adult responsibility. They are often treated like children and yet expected not to act childish. So, their vigilance about fairness is understandable. The problem is that their understanding of fairness is too simplistic. It is our job, as adults, to help them grasp a more mature understanding of fairness. But to do so, we must first develop a clear sense of what fairness means to us.

Contrary to popular convention, "fair" does not mean equal. Equal means everyone gets the exact same thing. Fair means everyone gets what they need. Certainly, equality is paramount in many situations. However, in some situations equality is not enough—or is even unfair. This concept may seem confusing or contradictory, so I offer the following as an illustration. In a crowded restaurant, a man begins to choke on a piece of food. The waiter says to him, "I know the Heimlich maneuver and would be happy to help you, but there are a lot of patrons here today and since I cannot offer the Heimlich to all of them, it would not be fair of me to offer it to you."

Most of us can easily see the absurdity in this situation. However, we find it more difficult to apply the same principle in more personal situations. In schools all across the country, teachers struggle with the concept of offering accommodations to students with special education needs. They feel that if *one* student is read a test aloud, then *all* students should be read the test aloud. However, all students do not have a reading disability and *need* the test read aloud in order to demonstrate what they have learned. These teachers fail to see that fairness is offering each student what is needed for *them* to learn. There are only three situations in which I agree that an accommodation is "unfair":

1. If it is offered to a student who does not *need* it
2. If it puts a student at a true advantage over other students
3. If it is not offered to all students who need it.

If you can state with integrity that the student receiving an accommodation needs it, that it levels the playing field and does not put the student at an advantage, and that you would do the same for any student with a similar need, then you are not being unfair. You are offering accommodations that simply allow a student to succeed.

Parents are not immune to falling into the trap of fairness either. One child in the family has hit a growth spurt and *needs* new clothes. The other *wants* new clothes and claims it is "unfair" that the sibling gets to go shopping and s/he does not. Or one child in a family is transported by a parent to a special education center and the other takes public transportation to public school. As long as you can look your children in the eye and state with assurance that you would do the same for them if they *needed* it, you should never feel that you have to do the exact same thing for every child in the family.

In my first year out of graduate school, I had the privilege of working with a group of severely troubled pre-adolescent boys in a special education setting. Each was so unique in his needs, strengths, and challenges that I found myself developing entirely different protocols for each one. One young man had a high level of anxiety in group situations and extreme difficulty simply remaining in the room during our group counseling sessions. So, in conversation with him, we agreed that he could remove himself from the circle and sit apart from the group when he became anxious, if he could try to stay in the room.

The first time he tried this accommodation, one of the other boys asked if he, too, could sit on the floor away from the group. I said no, and he proceeded to tell me that I was being "unfair." Suddenly the entire group of boys erupted with claims that I was unfair, offering examples of things others got that they did not. They used each other's accommodations as examples of my lack of fairness. As the tension built, I knew my response to this verbal attack would set a tone for the rest of the school year. So, I chose my response very carefully.

I let them rant and complain a little and then asked them to quiet down so I could respond. I told them that "fair" did not mean equal. Rather, it meant getting what you needed. I asked them not to think of what *others* were getting but to think about what I was doing to help *them.* I went around the circle and looked each and every boy in the eye and asked very sincerely, "Do you truly feel that I am not giving you what *you* need?" In turn, each kid fell silent and shook his head no (and I heaved a sigh of relief). Once or twice throughout that school year, we had to revisit the notion of fairness, but for the most part it was never again really an issue.

I urge you to grapple, if you must, with your own understanding of fairness and then help to teach the adolescents in your life that *fair is not equal and equal is not fair.*

Horses Don't Text

Horses can't text, but teenagers can, and do. Whether we understand and embrace the technology revolution or not, we have to acknowledge that it plays a prominent part in the lives of our teens. In some ways, texting is their language. We might not like it, but it does us no good to begrudge it. Many years ago, in my private practice with older teens I began using texting as a way of connecting with them. At the time, some of my professional colleagues questioned my judgment, feeling that this was not an appropriate means of communication between a therapist and client. My response was that I wanted to be open to the form of communication most comfortable for my client. In many cases, this was texting.

Certainly, my therapeutic approach involved more than just texting, but I was not afraid to enter their world and communicate in their language. In fact, doing so gave me an unexpected advantage. From the safety of a technology device, many teens were more expressive and spontaneous than they were in person. They tended to reach out more, because somehow it felt less threatening. Texting was certainly a useful tool for confirming appointments, but I came to see it as much more. It allowed me to unobtrusively let one of my clients know I was thinking of them, wishing them well, rooting for them, etc. It enabled me to maintain the connection between sessions and allowed some of my clients to hold onto the relationship in a way that spurred them toward further improvement.

My appreciation for the value of texting was irrevocably solidified in my work with Danny. Danny was a private client who had recently been kicked out of his private school placement for aggressive behavior. However, behind his aggression was a severe depression that had resulted in psychotic symptoms. He was having frequent thoughts of hurting himself and hearing voices that told him he should do so. Danny's mom had been advised by the school psychologist to hospitalize him, but was reluctant to do so. Danny had been hospitalized before with poor results. His mom felt motivated to put in place at home the safeguards that would support Danny through this difficult time. Key to the success of this plan would be Danny's cooperation.

The three of us sat down and developed a plan to get through the week one day at a time. The plan involved Danny's mom taking time off work to be with him, involving relatives to provide supervision and support when his mom could not be present, scheduling an emergency appointment with his psychiatrist and multiple sessions with me over the next few days, and frequent *texting*. In fact, texting was a critical part of the safety plan. You see, Danny might have been reluctant to *call* me or his mom and *say* that he was feeling unsafe, but he was perfectly willing to *text* us. And I could easily text Danny throughout the week and check in on him without being overly intrusive.

For the next week, Danny and I texted several times a day. We also saw each other several times and worked together to help Danny regain emotional stability. But the texting was the glue that helped maintain the connection between appointments. Many professionals might have felt that I was irresponsible in colluding with Danny's mom to develop a plan that prevented him from being hospitalized. And many would also seriously question my judgment in utilizing texting as a prominent part of a safety plan. However, I will continue to contend that with teenagers, reaching them in their own language and joining them in their own world is often the most therapeutic intervention we can offer.

I know of parents who have come to the same conclusion and have embraced the fact that their teen will share more information via text than conversation. The same teen who will offer a monosyllabic response to queries about his day at school, a date, or a big game is likely to text a whole lot more in response to the same questions. This might not make sense to you, but that doesn't make it wrong or any less true. So, I encourage parents to ask themselves, "Can I be open to the communication in whatever form it comes, or must I insist on verbal communication?"

Conclusion

If I have succeeded, you now have a significantly different perspective on adolescents than you did when you started to read this book. Through the discussion of how similar they are to horses, we have looked at teenagers in a new light. My aim is that you have a deeper understanding and a greater appreciation for their stage of development and the unique challenges they face. I hope that you feel better equipped to interact with them in an effective manner and that those interactions will no longer leave you frustrated and bewildered. My dream is that, as a society, we begin to shift our perspective of adolescents to one that truly appreciates and honors the challenges of their stage of development and supports them in their transition to young adults.

I believe that as science continues to inform us about the teenage brain and that as teens continue to use social media to insert themselves more and more into society, we will begin to see their inherent value and hear what they have to say; and we will take more seriously our responsibility in helping to shape them into the responsible and thoughtful adults they can be.

There is one final thing I would like you to take from this book. Teens *have important things to say!* And only by listening with an open mind and an open heart can we hope to bridge the gap between our adult world and theirs. Only through compassion and leadership can we form a connection based on mutual respect, earn their cooperation, and be deserving of their trust.

In the next section of this book, you will hear from teens directly, in their own words, about their own experiences of adolescence. Their stories are real—and their language may be raw. Some of the stories portray painful episodes in their lives where they battled depression or anxiety or struggled with sexuality. One writer captures the essence of adolescence through an adventure with friends. Another tells of a magical encounter with a horse. Yet another expresses the hardship of dealing with a parent's alcoholism. Together these young authors touch on learning disabilities, drug use, bullying, suicide, self-harm, eating disorders, and the deep unspoken need for parental guidance and support. They convey how confusing relationships are and how fragile self-esteem is during adolescence. Some of the stories may inspire tears and others offer profound insights, advice, or a thought-provoking perspective.

Tap into your kindred spirit and read their stories with an open mind. Read beyond the incorrect grammar and the occasional harsh tone. See past the curse words and grasp the depth of meaning. Hear what they have to say and appreciate the bravery it took to write each story. Take in their stories with an open heart and let them guide you in a better understanding of the adolescents in your life.

PART III

In Their Own Words...

Challenging Life's Challenges

Kylee Horstman
Age 18
Herndon, Virginia

Every teen has a story to tell. I don't like telling mine because I know that there are other people whose stories are worse. The only reason I chose to tell my story now is because I have been told that what I have gone through and experienced in my life definitely makes for something to be shared. One could say my story has taught me that everyone has challenges of their own to deal with and that everyone has his or her own story. I have learned that that doesn't mean my difficulties are any less important. Out of everything I have overcome, learning that I matter and that I am just as important as the next person has been the hardest battle—but the most valuable lesson. To this day, it is a battle I am still fighting through and learning from.

As far back as I can remember I have felt different, out of place, and anxious. I always wanted to have friends, to be able to impress those friends, and I needed to be my best for them. Unfortunately, making friends requires having enough confidence to be able to talk to a stranger. To impress someone, you have to have the guts to try something that will make you stand out from the rest and not constantly worry about messing up, failing, and making a fool of yourself. And lastly, being the best comes with being comfortable about how you feel and not letting others' feelings and opinions impact you.

I'm not saying to tune out others' feelings completely and show no understanding or sympathy for them, not at all. I am saying to be there for others, but at the same time, be there for you. With all of the anxiety I was experiencing, there was never time to be there for myself or care for me; eventually I forgot how. The challenge of my anxiety not only continued as I grew older, but it led to several other challenges I would have to face.

Another challenge in my story was the addition of two other mental illnesses—obsessive compulsive disorder (OCD) and depression. In second grade, I was diagnosed with OCD, after I had stolen several things and scribbled on a bathroom wall with markers. In my opinion, I had created a work of art, but my teacher and principal thought differently. When asked why I had done such things, I couldn't come up with a better reason than, "I had to." I knew it was wrong, but in the moment when a bad idea struck me, it felt like I couldn't *not* do it. I HAD to act on these kinds of thoughts and actions.

I later learned that I obsessed over certain thoughts, or what I could or wanted to do. I kept obsessing until I acted on that certain thought. I learned that when I acted on one of those thoughts, it was a compulsion. I then started seeing a therapist and taking medication. At age seven, I was on heavy medication, not really knowing what was wrong and what the medication was supposed to be doing.

While the therapist was great and got a pretty good handle on the OCD, no one realized that I was becoming depressed. In the eighth grade, I finally mentioned something to a teacher and then to my mom. The solutions at that point in time for a diagnosis of clinical depression were more therapy and more medication. These solutions handled these specific challenges but were no match for what was yet to come.

High school started just as things were beginning to even out. As if high school itself wasn't already a huge challenge, I had to face it while dealing with my own set of challenges, my mental illnesses. I had a couple of close friends in middle school but never a real group of friends, as everyone else seemed to have. When I entered high school, my anxiety reared its ugly head and I lost contact with the few good friends I had.

I then reconnected with an old one. While I was heartbroken about the friends I had lost, at times I could have cared less because of how quickly we reconnected and how close we soon became. We did absolutely everything together; I told her everything and she told me everything. We became so close that when someone would see one of us without the other, they actually became slightly worried. She was amazing, and I didn't care if I never made another friend, as long as I had her. This paradise of the two of us was all I would ever need because my anxiety, OCD, and depression became virtually nonexistent. Or so I thought.

I soon learned that my best friend came with troubles of her own and I, being the caring and compassionate person that I am, was there to listen. It turned out that I was also there to be yelled at, bullied, made fun of, and told how worthless I was. Throughout all of this, I began to grow strong feelings for her, but becoming anxious once again, I never acted on those feelings and missed the fact that she had them too.

When I finally realized we had a relationship that went beyond friendship, it was an emotionally abusive one. She told me that if we were going to stay in this relationship, I would have to change how I looked and how I acted because I was not good enough for her as myself. As terrible as it all was, I still loved my best friend. I loved her so much that I fell in love with her. The abuse continued, and instead of stepping up and saying something, I stepped back and let my mental disorders take over.

I became extremely anxious whenever I was around her, for fear that I might do something wrong and have to experience her ferocious rage. I was always checking and rechecking what I was doing and saying in order to please her, never thinking about myself. And as her comments and insults became much stronger, my self-esteem became much weaker. No matter what anyone says, if you are told enough times that you are ugly, stupid, and annoying; you will start to believe him or her. If all of that was not grounds for clinical depression and a poor self-image and self-esteem, then I don't know what is.

About halfway through my junior year of high school, I finally found the courage and strength to break all ties with my best friend and to move on with my life. As many people know, moving on with one's life is always easier said than done. The rest of that school year was the absolute worst period of my life. While breaking up with her and losing our friendship was the best decision I could have made at the time, it felt like the worst.

Leaping to the complete opposite side of the spectrum, my senior year of high school was without a doubt the best time of my life. While I was still severely anxious and depressed most days, I battled through it with the help of my new friends; friends I never thought I would make and friends I never want to lose. I had acquired a new, close set of friends and was welcomed among a larger group of my fellow classmates than I had ever been before.

One of the reasons I loved that year so much was because I learned that my new friends had experienced what I had experienced and continued to suffer from what I suffered from; and they had found a great way to fix it. Their answer to the challenges of living was alcohol. I liked alcohol and soon fell in love with it. I found alcohol especially helpful for me because it erased my social anxiety and made connecting with others really easy. Most importantly, I relearned that it was okay to talk to and confide in friends and family and they wouldn't judge or mock you.

When I was busy stumbling around wasted and talking to everyone about who knows what, it was impossible to worry about myself, or what people thought of me or my life in general. Alcohol made me happy, and no amount of medication in the world had been able to do that. Unfortunately for me, when you start drinking with the intention to forget your worries and problems, you instead forget why you started drinking in the first place. I may have learned some healthy coping strategies during my senior year, such as my daily routine of talking to my friends, going to school, being around people I know and trust, and being able to fall back on my parents, but my one unhealthy strategy was enough to bring them all tumbling down. As my ways to cope in a healthy manner disappeared with the start of college, I fell back on my poor coping skill of drinking.

As much as parents, especially my parents, hate to admit it, college life revolves around partying, not education. While the latter is definitely important, it comes second to the social scene. A good social scene can always be found around a good party. And if you haven't already guessed it, a lot of people and a lot of alcohol can be found around a lot of good parties. Seeing as how I have more social anxiety than I know what to do with, people tend to be a problem for me, especially when I have to actually be around them. Luckily, I fixed that problem with alcohol—a lot of alcohol that usually ended up being too much.

The alcohol solution worked so well that it completely rid me of any and all anxiety, allowing me to enjoy normal social interactions. I didn't realize until much later that it also allowed me to enjoy dangerous social situations that I would have never been in before. I talked to people I never would have spoken to, I became involved with sex and drugs, I woke up in strangers' houses, and blacked out so often that I still can't remember where I may have been or what I may have done. I was able to rationalize the bad experiences, and I kept drinking in order to become numb and cope with my life.

As if the drinking wasn't enough of a challenge, being away at school gave way to two other poor coping strategies. The first dealt with my self-esteem and body image; both of these were so bad that I decided to stop eating. While I didn't stop eating altogether, I only ate what I would need to get through each day in one piece. Going through a day with only a Pop-Tart for breakfast, a soda for lunch, and then some crackers for dinner was hard and sometimes painful. All of that hardship and pain disappeared, though, when I could count one more rib or see that I had lost one more pound. With as much alcohol as I was drinking and as much medication as I was taking, eating so little was extremely unhealthy, extremely dangerous, and extremely stupid.

I then began to self-injure. Being too anxious to talk to anyone at school, convincing myself that my other friends away at their colleges had better things to do, and fearing that my parents were already probably worried sick about me, I kept all of my emotions locked inside. Having so much anger, self-doubt, and sadness inside of you for long enough can destroy you. I know it destroyed me. The only way I knew to express how I was feeling inside was to drink and cut myself when even the alcohol wasn't enough.

Contrary to popular belief, you don't feel pain when you self-injure; most people feel pleasure. The anticipation of the blade slicing across your skin, the sight of the bright red blood as it flows down your wrist, and the cut itself all bring the most wonderful rush of endorphins. That rush of adrenaline is the closest thing I had to feeling happy. As time went on, it was the closest thing I had to feeling anything at all. I was descending into a dark place that I had never been in and never thought I would get out of.

I knew I had a problem—well, several problems if we're going to get technical. But I didn't really accept that fact until after two events. One event consisted of me landing myself in the hospital because of an accidental overdose. Before a party one night, I decided that I needed to get super-drunk super-fast, because it had been a rough day. I figured the best way to do that was to take an extra dose of my daily medication. As stated before, parties involve a lot of alcohol and I love alcohol. Unfortunately, alcohol and antidepressants don't mix, especially if you take more than prescribed. Even after waking up alone, strapped to a hospital bed, scared out of my mind, and not knowing whether I had been drugged or taken advantage of, I didn't accept that something needed to change, until after the second event.

I still continued to drink after my lovely stay in the hospital, and it became apparent how bad of an idea it was, after I cut myself while I was drunk. I was lucky and didn't go too deep, and I was blessed that I had a roommate who cared enough to help make sure I was okay, even though I must have scared and scarred her. Needless to say, it was time for me to take a break from school, college, and partying, and focus on myself and the challenges I needed to overcome.

As much as I wish it did, going home and talking to a therapist did not fix the problems as quickly as I would have liked. To be completely honest, the problems still aren't fixed, and it is now seven months since the overdose—after leaving school early, finding a therapist, considering suicide, going to another party, getting way too drunk, having a twelve-day stay in a mental institution, attending AA meetings, taking the following semester off from college, deciding to transfer colleges, taking so many medication changes that I have lost count, and finally accepting the diagnosis of six different mental illnesses.

While all of this time and all of these things haven't fixed my problems, they have definitely helped them. I have been free of alcohol for five months; I talk to my therapist on a regular basis; I am on medicine that allows me to have more good days than bad ones; and I can actually say that I have experienced happiness. And happiness is the one thing I needed and still need so desperately.

Happiness is the one thing that everyone needs. Happiness is also the thing that some people have no problem finding and holding on to. For others, it can be a huge problem; for someone who suffers from one or more mental disorders it may seem nearly impossible. I know it did, and on some days, it still does for me.

While I am supposed to be writing about a challenge I overcame, I'm writing about one I am still working on overcoming. I also threw in several completed challenges that I couldn't be more proud of. I know that with time and with my great friends and support system, I will overcome the challenge of my mental illnesses and attain a life full of happiness.

Happiness

Kelly Dodd
Age 17
Chantilly, Virginia

This is a story about finding happiness. My friend once told me that I live life on fast forward, whether it's jumping off a waterfall or sitting in a hospital watching loved ones tangled in tubes and wires, and I thank God that I live such a life. Yet, I was not always thankful for this fact.

A story is best told from the beginning, and my beginning is spring break, junior year, at a friend's home in London. My life felt as if it was falling apart, but I was used to that. I had accepted that life doses misfortune at random, and I simply had poor luck. My life was tangled from a young age with an uncontrollable series of sick family, suicidal friends, and a parent with an unfortunate love of wine and distaste towards food. So there I was, walking down Oxford Street in my favorite leather boots, feeling myself all together sorrier than usual for a particularly unfortunate start to 2012—a second divorce for my mother that sent her on a few trips to the hospital. During this time, I found comfort by escaping into the world of costuming or through the pages of John Green's novel, *Looking for Alaska*.

Later in the school year, I began to worry. I had always believed that I could survive any hardship, as long as I felt emotion. I felt myself closing off, separating myself from my friends, feeling less every day, and realizing that even my favorite novelist couldn't draw an ounce of emotion from my hardening heart. I had hit rock bottom.

But as I said, this is a story about finding happiness. Jump to August, two weeks before coming home from an eight-week program at Stanford. This is where I found the secret to happiness. It isn't about perfection, tests, security, or even love. It is realizing that the world is chaotic. For me, happiness was found when I stopped watching others' lives and I began to live my own life. I began to listen to different languages, learn new ways to smile, push my intellectual limits, and discover that silly jokes such as balancing spoons on noses can sometimes be the best thing about a day.

In the end, the secret to happiness is to be willing to accept the chaos and try to find a new piece of yourself or the world every day that brings joy. Then, when there is a reason to be sad, you can remember that there will always be more smiles and more laughs coming your way.

Misery Loves Her Sister

Madisen Norton
Age 16
Littleton, Colorado

It was sometime in October when she started to lose herself; the month that destroyed my life. The leaves on the trees were falling, and the wind blew them around in a colorful tornado. I noticed she was rude, and I just assumed that she was being a disrespectful teenager. I was wrong. She was a disrespectful, pompous, ignorant teenager. I had gone through the very same phase, until someone told me to get my head out of my ass and learn some respect. She had people telling her the same thing; I was one of them. It still wasn't enough.

The smile she always wore was gone, replaced with an unfriendly pout. She walked into school slumped over. I assumed that she was weighed down by her heavy textbooks. I was wrong about that too. Somehow, she had changed. Over the course of a couple weeks, she had turned into a person almost everyone hated. Even me—I hated her too. I shouldn't have, because it wasn't her fault.

Her mascara was smeared around her eyes, making her appear like a corpse. The dark circles didn't really help her appearance either. I gave her some fancy cream that I'd gotten from a gift bag that should have helped. She didn't use it. She stopped caring about grades, she didn't spend much time primping in front of the mirror, and she started ditching swim practice. *What has happened to you?* The thought echoed through my mind as I looked at that girl. *Why have you done this?* I missed the memory of the kid she had been. I really did.

She used to have those bangs that were chopped straight across her face; it made her hazel eyes look even bigger. She was a deer child, perhaps. She didn't walk, she bounded. She didn't run, she frolicked. She shared my love of cats, any and every kind. She was the kid who saved worms from the sidewalk and put them back in the grass. When we were little, we would perch in tall pine trees and collect the cones that had fallen on the ground.

"Yum, a mouse!" I would say, pretending that all the pinecones we found at the base of our tree were the equivalent of food, and of course, I would meow and she would meow too. That's what cats say. Then, we would climb back up our tree—each of us sat on our assigned perch, and that's how we spent our time. In the fall, we buried our pinecones so that we would have something for our cat identities to eat over the winter. She wanted the fat and open pinecones, the ones with the color that was just a shade darker than her hair, claiming that, "these mice taste better than the other mice." Around October, we would sit up in our pine tree and watch the leaves soar around in the wind.

She ruined fall.

After school, we start our daily routine; she gets in the car silently, with her eyes glazed over as they always are now, and she manages not to look at me. She doesn't look at anyone really. She keeps her head down most of the time. And then I try to have a conversation, because I'm not a fan of silence—just like I do every single day.

"How was your day?"

"Fine."

"That's good. Did you do well on the science test?"

"I don't know."

"Well, how do you think you did?"

"I don't know. "

"Was it hard?"

"Not really."

"Then maybe you did well."

"Maybe…"

She shrugs off her backpack and fishes around in one of the front pouches until she finds those iPhone headphones that are covered in Sharpie and blasts some song by a band called Five Finger Death Punch. I don't say anything about being able to hear the music across the car. I assume that she's had a rough day and that maybe she needs to blast away her worries with angry men screaming. I was wrong. I won't be able to listen to metal again.

She was always the social butterfly, making friends almost anywhere, even with a girl at the beach in Florida. Our families bonded and we spent the rest of vacation with them. The two of them played in the sand, making elaborate houses for the imaginary friends they both shared. I envied her ability to make friends. While she would bond with strangers, I would walk along the beach and look for those twisty seashells.

It should be me, the one who is alone, but somehow over the years, the tables turned. Now, she walks across campus, behind people who were previously her friends. Not next to them, but behind them. She halfway tries to catch up to them, halfway trips over the sneakers she's drawn all over. She barks out a bitter laugh that shouldn't belong to her.

She stopped walking to the parking lot so I could pick her up. Now, I have to drive around to the place on campus where I know she'll be. She sits on the old brick wall by the art building with the really loud fan, alone. Rumor has it that a boy in first grade was pushed on the fan by his friends; he evidently lost his pinky finger. She sees the car and takes her time waltzing over. She yanks on the door, which I forgot to unlock, and gets an annoyed look on her face. Actually, thinking about it, she has more of an annoyed pout. I investigate.

"Hey."

"Hi."

"How was your day?"

"Fine."

"Just fine?"

"Yeah."

"What's wrong?"

"Nothing."

"It has to be something."

"It's not, shut up please."

"That's rude. I think that you should talk. It's called a conversation."

"Well, I don't feel like talking."

"Then I hope you're okay with walking home."

"Yeah, maybe I'll call Mom and tell her about the science test that you flunked."

"Maybe I already told her."

"Maybe you should go..."

And then the car honks behind us, interrupting the swear-off that was about to ensue. In the rearview mirror, I see it's one of the "mommies," as we call them. They are the parents who only care about themselves and their "academically gifted" children. At this point, I'm seriously considering backing up a couple of inches and scratching the paint on her stupid sparkly Escalade. But I don't. That's the difference between the two of us—I have self-control. She doesn't.

"I hate them," she says. Her eyes are down and the look of anger has passed over her face, replaced with something dejected.

"I hate them too."

Things only got worse for her. Her comments got snappier, and her behavior was inexcusable. Teachers at school walked up to me, asking if there was any problem with her at home. Mom finally got fed up with her and took her to a counselor, an all-family counselor. It was an attempt to keep her on track and maybe solve her problem. Her problem was bigger than Mom, way bigger than any of us.

How did I think she felt about the counselor? He irritated even me.

"So, how do you feel about your sister's recent behavior?"

"What kind of question is that? How do I feeeeeel about it?"

"Obviously you're upset."

"No shit, Sherlock. I don't want to tell you how I feel. You know damn well how I feel. It sucks, and I just want her back."

"I understand. But your emotions are getting the better of you. I think that this problem is affecting you more than you thi—"

"You have no clue what this has done to my family. You can't even fathom how hard this is. Stop pretending you do. This isn't helping."

And then I get up and walk out of his office, adding a very appropriate teenager slam of the door as I exit. Mom gives me a degrading look that I deserve, and together we leave the facility. She is already in the car, headphones in her ears, and she is no doubt blasting some angry rock song.

She's by the fan again. I notice that she is wearing one of my shirts; the black one with the little monster that glows in the dark. She didn't ask to use it.

"Hey, I don't remember you asking to wear my shirt."

"I didn't. You wore my sports bra without asking. This is how you are repaying me."

"No, that was my sports bra."

"It was mine. Stop being a liar."

"Fine, whatever. You're wrong, but whatever. How was your day?"

"Fun."

"That's good."

And then I notice it, the drawing on her wrist. It's a pair of scissors, with a long dotted line that extends across the length of her wrist. It is the drawing that you notice as a kid, the drawing after the teacher hands out safety scissors and some kind of craft that involves glitter glue. It means "cut along this line." Cut along her wrist.

"Um…"

"What?"

"What is that drawing?"

"What drawing?"

"The scissors on your wrist! What the Hell?! Do you want to die?!"

She gives me this look, some kind of brew of anger and evil and sadness all smeared on the face of somebody that I used to love. The car is silent on the way home. She isn't listening to her angry music; she sits with her head turned away and stares out the window.

About a week later, I go into her room, looking for the shirt that she stole from me. I see the baby blue walls and the giant ice cream lamp that some relative got for her. That was something she used to love—candy and sweets and baked goods. How did she outgrow that too? I call her name, because going into her room is against the law. Back in the day, I could let myself in to steal some make-up, and now she insists that my actions need to be witnessed. I find the violated shirt on the floor in her bathroom. It has some kind of toothpaste all over it. Feeling irritated, I stand up and look into the mirror. The word freak is written across the surface in a burgundy lip color. Lipstick is something that she ruined as well, something that I won't be able use for a while. I exit the room as fast as I can, leaving the soiled shirt behind.

"Mom?"

"Yeah? I'm in my room."

"I'm worried about her."

"I am too. Are you sure nothing is going on at school?"

"No. I'm not sure. I have no idea anymore."

And then the two of us have one of those awkward hugs, and I burst into tears and let all my confusion and anger run down my face. I sit in my bed crying and hoping that things will turn around, that she will turn herself around.

Sometime in November, I got a text from her. It said, "Hey, no need to pick me up, getting a ride from a friend." And I replied with an "okay have fun☒." I went home and was happy that she finally bonded with someone and was going to have a girls' night. The phrase "things are looking up" kept playing through my head, and I even sang along to the radio.

Later that night in November, she didn't come home. I called her and she didn't answer. I called Mom and told her that she was with a friend and that she hadn't come home yet. I called any possible friend that she could have been with. No one had seen her. I called Mom again and she lost her mind, crying and yelling and sounding not at all surprised. I shouldn't have been surprised either.

I stayed up all night, that night in November. I scanned the street, the front door, and any other place where she could arrive and say that she wanted to come home. She wouldn't, and she didn't. By dawn, the police were searching. They interviewed me, Mom, the neighbors, her teachers, and anyone else they could reach at four in the morning. Then, they went into the woods behind our house. Our woods.

The back of my throat locks and everything starts to make sense. And then…

I wear black. Everyone does. And I'm walking up a long aisle to a microphone. I focus on my steps, one foot in front of the other. *Don't trip over your heels.* And I know I'm supposed to say the words that I wrote down on a piece of paper and say them without crying. Other people are crying, people who are related, people who went to school with her, her coaches. I'm not. I can't.

"Hey kid. I love you and I hope you know that. And I'm sorry that you weren't happy and I hope you are in a place where you found peace."

And then I step down after my lame-ass speech, more like a lame-ass sentence. That wasn't all I had to say, not even close. I didn't do her justice.

It's December. And it's snowing and cold and gray. It matches my mood almost perfectly. Winter is always particularly depressing. I'm happy that autumn is over. It made me sick for a while. I can't listen to any songs that have a very aggressive guitar solo or any songs that involve any screaming; I just turn off the radio. The fan by the art room gives me a migraine. I avoid it at all costs.

Sometime later in December, I work up some courage and decide that I need closure. I put on my waterproof boots and a heavy sweater and decide to take a stroll in the woods. I grab some tissues; I'll need them. The snow isn't too deep and it isn't particularly cold, but I'm still numb. I pass all the baby pine trees, the little stream where we played in the summer, and the rusty shovel that someone forgot to pick up. They were all a part of the memories. *Keep going. Only a few more paces until you get there.* I don't need my mind to guide me. The path is automatic.

And then I get there, to the pine tree with the thick branches that could handle a kid jumping on them, that could handle a kid swinging from them, that could handle a kid hanging from them. And of course I'm glad I brought those tissues because I collapse against the trunk and curl into a fetal position and am oddly happy that she died in such a beautiful place. But I'm not actually happy. *How can I be?*

I pick up one of those perfect pinecones, the ones with no broken spikes, and with the color a shade darker than her hair, and I put it in my pocket. I have to leave, because I have a test in the morning and I have to study. I notice that it's really hard to pick myself up and that my muscles are tense, and I don't want to leave. I want to stay with her.

Somehow life goes on. Kind of. I'm not a fan of lipstick, and the image of her mirror is enough to make me sick, and I feel obligated to wipe it off. The fall is always brutal, and I go into two months of silence and solitude, the months of October and November. I don't eat candy on Halloween and I don't eat Thanksgiving dinner; it doesn't seem fair to her. And I can't say her name. I can't write it or hear it because it conjures up all of these horrible things that I have tried so very hard to forget.

At Christmas, I don't comment on all the pinecones that are set up around the house. They make me kind of happy actually; this is the holiday that she got to spend with us.

Mom is on some kind of antidepressant, but Christmas always seems to get her out of that funk. We eat dinner and open presents and sing songs and bake and do all the normal Christmas things. And somehow life goes on. But not really.

I go to school every day and see the people, the people who killed her. They are the people who said things and did things that ruined her spirit. And I wish that it was them who had to watch as their sister self-destructed, and feel guilty for not being able to fix it, and cry because their best friend is dead.

Their lives go on. And my life goes on. But not really.[1]

1. Please Note: This story was originally published under the same title in *The Burning Page*, 2012-2013.

To My Parents

A.S.
Age 19
Silver Spring, Maryland

Mom. Dad.

I thought I learned what love was in the stalls of the girls' bathroom my sophomore year of high school. I thought it was cutting class just to talk and roam around the school. Throwing food and insults across the lunchroom table, apologies etched with sincerity delivered to her locker the next day. I thought there was something there, because my days smiled five times brighter when I heard her voice. I thought it was in the forgiveness of my clumsy and rough self, where I spilled juice on her brand new shoes and followed the outdated unethical schoolyard tradition of hurting someone when you like them. I thought there was love in the acceptance of my sometimes tough self. Even though I meant to be kinder, my mouth and sometimes my hands forgot.

I wish you had told me bruises don't mean love or even "like" and that I'm wrong, not because she's not a "he," but because I'm too young to be worried about any of this. I wish

I could've asked you about her, because I understood biology just fine but I had no clue what was happening when it came to the fluttering in my chest and the shakiness of my hands when she smiled.

Mom. Dad.

I thought I knew what love was when I sat with her on my friend's couch, while everyone else was asleep at three in the morning, and shared secrets I had never told anyone else. In the darkness, we found out our scars matched, and after months of "don't scream, don't cry," it was refreshing to see someone look at my arms and wonder "why?"—and it felt crucial that she was the first person to ask.

For months, I thrived on pretty words and shy laughter and was protected by razors and ignorance, a hug a day and a kind word every now and again.

I couldn't ask you why being around her was too much and not enough.

I wish I could've told you, because I needed you that day, second semester senior year. After I read my story to the class about the two little girls who had fallen in love even though it hurt, I was met with nothing but support. I walked into lunch next period, silently triumphant, and I sat down to eat, and she reached for my hand without a second thought, and I swear it was like holding the tether to thousands of balloons, because I was flying when she smiled at me.

But it broke when these girls from class played some fucked up version of Spin the Bottle without my consent and sent over a freshman to confess her imaginary love for me. In the middle of the cafeteria, I stopped flying and these girls were too busy laughing to notice. With the snickers and whispers a few tables down, no one had to remind me to keep a stiff upper lip, even though I'm sure my eyes watered a bit. I'm glad my friends pretended they didn't see, but suddenly my tether felt more like an anchor, because I wanted to do nothing more than drop her hand and run. When the freshman walked away and they told me I should go after her to make sure she was all right, I wish I could've told you so that someone would've cared if *I* was all right.

The bell rang and I let go of her hand, because I didn't feel like trying to fly anymore. I haven't held it since.

I wish I could've told you. Maybe then I would've believed I wasn't wrong in staying put and not making a fuss, even though all kinds of *awful* exploded inside. Maybe I would've believed that when the scene was replayed in class next period, I didn't have to laugh along with everyone else.

Maybe I would've gotten the courage to hold her hand again.

Mom. Dad.

I was positive this was love because I didn't know when it started. There was never shame in the hand I grasped or worry in the words I whispered and sometimes even shouted. Time with her was all one hallelujah that made me feel like salvation was promised every day.

Because even though the depression talked me up to the edge of a twenty-story building every day, she would grab my hand and walk me back down.

I wish I could've told you. Maybe you would've warned me that this couldn't last. And that everyone saves each other until we can't. And on the day she wouldn't be able to, I shouldn't blame her for being stuck. Instead, I should ask her why she's always already on the roof, waiting with her feet dangling off the edge.

Mom. Dad.

My friends told me this was love when they threw away my razors and begged me to see the doctor for the voices I kept hearing. They told me to come to them if I wanted to talk. I ignored them because I wanted you. I wanted to talk to you but believed I couldn't because you might not have loved me anymore if I did.

So I learned to keep my silence. But sometimes, it became too heavy and too much and I had to let some of it go. Sometimes, I still look at my arms to see how much sadness I've tried to spill out.

Mom. Dad.

Back then is when I needed you to accept me in a way I could recognize. I needed to know I had open arms that welcomed whoever I was and whoever I would be, without judgment. I didn't know if I had it. Sometimes I still don't.

But that's okay.

I know we didn't talk enough for us to really know each other. I'll tell you my stories if you want to hear them, and I'd like to hear yours.

Mom. Dad.

I'm starting the conversation.

But before we share stories, can you tell me what love is? I'm tired of getting it wrong.

Redwolf

Delilah Schweitzer
Age 14
Middletown, Maryland

You can learn a lot from animals. They're wise, playful, loving, and sometimes more forgiving than humans. It probably has to do mostly with the fact that they haven't been corrupted by mankind. But, we can still watch them and see how they run things. And maybe, just maybe one day, this society can learn a thing or two from them.

Take wolves, for example. They work, live, and *breathe* as a pack. They know how to work together. They know how to play together. They feed and care for each other even more than human families do.

There's a strict hierarchy to a wolf pack. There's the alpha male and female, who give the orders and expect no objection. And 9.9 out of 10 times, they get none. The others in the pack know that the alphas just do what's best for them. Everybody knows their role in the pack, and everybody respects that. With humans, it's not like that. There's always, *al-*

ways going to be someone somewhere disagreeing with what you say. That's just how this world works.

I once went into an enclosure with five wolves. Granted, it wasn't at a zoo. But, it was at a sanctuary. And, what do you know!! When you're not posing a threat or holding a gun and shooting at them, wolves are pretty darn social. All I had to do was look them in the eye and smile. Which is more than some do with other humans. Heck, I'm even guilty for not always looking people in the eye when I speak to them. It's just intimidating and makes you feel like they'll start judging you.

With the wolves, I knew that no matter what I had done previously in my life, or what I will end up doing, they didn't care. All that mattered was that I was sitting there calmly, looking them in the eyes and appearing friendly. And some of them came right up to me and licked my teeth! And they didn't have bad breath because they didn't eat processed meat.

Being a dog is much like being a teenager, I assume. For both, you're somewhat expected to take on the role society lays out for you. When you're a dog, you are expected to be cute and friendly. You're expected to be able to do some cute trick. But, in reality, not all dogs are cute or friendly to all human beings. And in reality, some dogs can't roll over or play dead. It's how things are.

When you're a teenager, you're supposed to be a rebel who hates your parents' guts and wishes they'd just *leave you alone!* But, in reality, not *all* teens hate their parents. Not all teens go against everything their parents say. I'm one of those teens. I love my parents and would never do something outrageously bad. I get good grades. I follow directions. Sure, some of my friends do repeatedly tell me stupid things their parents do or say. But, that's just human nature. *Everybody makes mistakes.*

Animals learn from their parents. Each parent teaches their baby an important aspect of their future life. In the human world, the equivalent of that would be teachers. The job of a teacher is to, well, teach us something that we will need later in life. Teachers and our parents help shape the person we are.

Yelling at us when we do something wrong doesn't really help. It just makes it worse. Sometimes, I wish that I *wasn't* human. Not just because animals have it better, but because of some of the complete *idiots* I unfortunately have to share the title of human with. I mean, seriously, people!

Another reason I'm often daydreaming of being an animal is that love is complicated at this age. It's weird because you might not like someone, but all your friends are in a relationship. And, a lot of relationships end badly. When you're an animal, whether you mate for life, or just reproduce and then move on, there are no hard feelings. It's just the way life is, and always will be.

And last time I checked, animals don't mercilessly kill each other in the thousands over some petty feud over land. I mean, sure, they fight and kill each other. But, that's nature! Taking guns and recruiting people to fight in wars is *not* nature. I hope for our sake, and the sake of the future generations, that our society can learn to love and care for one another as animals do.

My Story with Horses

Ziding Zhou
Age 17
Centennial, Colorado

Actually, I have not had many experiences with horses, but the experiences I have had have been enough to shape them in my mind and my heart, and also enough for me to give a good explanation about them to people who do not actually understand horses. I do not have many beautiful words or fantastic sentences to describe this wonderful group of animals, but I can promise that my poor vocabulary is enough to show how wonderful they actually are and make some impact on adults' thoughts about them.

My first thought of horses, as I can remember, was the summer of my fourth grade year. It was not the first time I saw an actual horse, but it was the first time that I was so close to a horse to know that this friend had a body at least two times bigger than me. He was a beautiful purplish-red wild horse, with a pair of big brown eyes. He galloped on the grassland of Inner Mongolia, which is located on the northern boundary of China. I was on a trip with my family during that summer.

In a late afternoon, I got lost. As the night came, the moon and the twinkling stars began coming out in the dark sky. I could not find my parents, and I did not know where I was. I just stood there in what was probably the center of the vast grassland of Inner Mongolia. I had my little mobile phone, which had no signal at all, and I put on my headphones. As I remember, I was surprisingly calm. I sat on the grass and listened to the music from my phone.

Suddenly, I heard a neigh, and it was not far away from me. I started to feel nervous. I had seen horses before, but I did not know how to deal with wild horses at all. Just as what I thought it was, this purplish-red wild horse appeared in the dark and kept coming towards me. I stood there, without moving. I was scared because I did not know what to do and I did not know what the horse might do to me. However, in less than one minute, I literally found that I was totally wrong about feeling scared of this meek wild horse.

He stopped right in front of me, and we looked at each other with both curiousness and fear. After a while—and this was the most surprising moment—he sat down right next to me and meekly put his head down on my feet. I was surprised. He was so much bigger than me and he was a wild horse—the kind of animal adults always tell us are dangerous and warn us that we better not to try to approach.

It was a chilly night, even though it was during the summer. I jumped onto his back and crossed my arms around his neck. He began walking. I did not know where he was trying to take me, but I felt a very deep trust as I sat on him. I did not know why I trusted this "dangerous," "strange" big horse, and even now I cannot find the reason that made me trust him so completely. He kept walking. And how surprising! I could never have believed what happened if I had not experienced it myself. Up ahead, I saw the yurts that I lived in. He took me home! This "stranger" took me home. He did not enter the yurt zone, but he kneeled down in the grass and let me get down from his back.

As soon as I got to the ground, there was a light; it seemed like a flashlight that appeared among the yurts. He stood up quickly and neighed again, and then he ran away. After several seconds, he disappeared into the darkness. I saw him the next morning, and I tried run to him, but the tour guide stopped me. She said, "Do not approach that wild horse...he may hurt you."

No, he wouldn't. He definitely wouldn't.

That was my first experience with a horse, and it makes me never feel afraid of horses anymore. Last summer, I came to United States for the rest of my high school year of study. There is a difference between American high school and Chinese high school—community service hours are required in American high schools. I needed thirty hours of community service as a junior. From the many community service websites, I chose a rescue ranch for horses. I am kind of like a super fan of horses. I love holding them on their necks and sitting on their backs. I know they will take me anywhere I want to go. Moreover, that purplish-red wild horse is still galloping in my mind.

The ranch where I volunteered was a big ranch, with more than thirty horses. Those horses had all been rescued from danger or adopted from poor families who had no abilities to raise them anymore. People working at the ranch showed us around and introduced my work to me. I signed up for office work on Sunday afternoons, so I did not have many times to spend with horses. But during my work breaks, I always left the office to enjoy the pretty sunshine and go to the place where the horses were. I always stood in front of the fence, because I was not allowed to go beyond it to touch the horses.

On the ranch, these horses were living happily and people took good care of them. They were treated as part of the family, like a growing child in their parents' eyes. Sometimes, I fed them grass and carrots that the ranch owner gave me. I touched them carefully and softly. They were quiet and just ate their food. I loved the time that I spent with them, and I love jobs that take care of horses.

Because of the experience I had with them and what else I've heard about them, I have decided that if I have the capability, I would like to be a zoologist or a professional animal protector. Some horses, or animals, are living happily under the protection of warmhearted people, but there are still many unfortunate horses suffering from abuse and hunting. They need help, and they need people to love them as they love people.

For me, horses are not "animals" or a kind of creature that exists in a lower order than human beings. They are part of the family—one of the friends. Horses also need a family, which loves them and protects them all the time; horses also need friends who really understand them and take care of them. They are not the dangerous creatures of parents' warnings, and if you try to get close to them and use your heart to understand them, you will realize how wonderful and friendly they are.

Dear parents and teachers, these meek, friendly horses won't eat your kids and they will not hurt them either. If you try to understand them or walk into their life politely and with full respect, they will pay you back with their love and their hearts. They just need people to understand them and not judge them as dangerous creatures or treat them awful by abusing them. They need a family with amiable parents and loving friends, but not abuse and misunderstanding.

Give yourself a chance, to understand and to love.

Moving Up the Staircase

Steven A. Howard
Age 25
Springfield, Virginia

What's it like to be a teenager? Well, it was both the best time of my life and the worst. I remember being in elementary school and thinking that high school kids were terrible. They were selfish, horny, and mean. I hoped that I could just skip the teenage years and go straight to becoming an adult. Unfortunately, I had to go through puberty first.

My trouble started in middle school. This was way back in the day when, if the County Department of Public Schooling knew you were disabled, they stuck you in a special class or a school for special needs until they figured out what to do with you. Most of the kids in my middle school were classified as emotionally disabled (ED for short), whereas, I was classified as learning disabled (LD for short)—although, for the record, I am also diagnosed with Tourette's syndrome and Asperger's.

My classmates had difficulty discerning emotions from other people, and in some cases, they had issues discerning their own. I did not have those kinds of issues. My biggest problem was reading a hand clock. Even now, at age twenty-five, I have issues reading it. The other day, a coworker discovered my dark secret and made it her quest to teach me this method of telling time. For twenty minutes, she tried to explain it to me. I just wasn't getting it. Deep down I knew that if the teacher, who has a Ph.D. in education, had issues helping me understand, then how was this person who hasn't even graduated high school gonna teach me? Eventually, I pretended that I'd had an epiphany and could read the hand clock. People still try to help me, or worse, tease me.

Teasing was my biggest issue in grade school, and more so in middle school, when telling time became harder to look past, since most kids my age could tie their shoes and count by twos and were expected to read a hand clock. There was one kid in my class who teased me every day about reading a hand clock, yet he could not even read the alphabet. But somehow he could look at a clock and tell me what time it was—and be correct. My mother always made things easier to understand, but even she couldn't explain a hand clock. Yet, she could explain the learning curve better to me than any college professor ever did.

"Son," she said to me, "kids learn one step at a time. But some kids, like you, don't walk up the stairs at the same pace as everyone else. Some kids stay on that one step until they are comfortable. Then, they race up twenty steps and wait for everyone else to catch up, since it's lonely up there. Once everyone else catches up, they wait until they're comfortable again and race up another twenty steps. They will repeat this process even after they reach college."

The staircase theory continues to weave intricately through my life even today. For example; I cannot drive a car, and I am twenty-five years old. It's not because I'm medically unable to do so; I'm just scared, which in many ways is how kids feel when they're learning math. All those crazy numbers and symbols you're supposed to read and know and comprehend! However, I know that this fear will pass, because I'm getting more comfortable on my staircase. When I'm good and ready, I'll probably not only drive, but become a racecar driver. To be fair, though, the racecar bit is probably an over-exaggeration, but who knows?

My father always said, "I don't care how bad you do. So long as you give it your best shot, I'll be proud of you." I find that having this attitude with kids who try hard encourages them to try harder, and who knows? They might even do better ultimately.

I volunteer at a summer camp for kids with cognitive disabilities. At that camp, it is common for kids to bring schoolwork. They're expected to work for an hour or two during times when the camp has no scheduled activities. Offering positive reinforcement and encouragement helps a lot. Even for the occasional F+. Some kids get F's because they slack off a lot and don't get any work done. Kids with disabilities may also do this, and they should not be exempt from punishment just because they are disabled. But kids who genuinely put all their effort into what they do and still get an F are more deserving of a reward of some kind than the kids who put little or no effort into it.

My father also has a saying, "lower expectations." He usually only uses this for watching movies, especially when there is so much hype about the movie ahead of time. But it is applicable anywhere actually. The idea is that if you go into a movie (or a situation) expecting it to REALLY SUCK, then when it surpasses your expectations you will be completely blown away. Alternatively, if it actually does REALLY SUCK, then you won't be too disappointed. More importantly your hopes won't be shattered.

This method can work to turn certain situations more positive. For instance, I know a guy who I hang out with occasionally. One day, he was taking a breather and a girl walked up to him and started flirting with him. He clearly was unaware of what she was doing, and I realized he was unable to read the social queues. So, I lowered my expectation and offered my support. When the girl left, I informed him that she was "totally into you" and gave him some pointers on how to read the signs in the future. Although I am hopeful he will succeed, I understand that he might not get it.

So what does all of this have to do with being a teenager? Well, everything really. Teenagers aren't born in the middle of the staircase. They start where everyone else starts—at the bottom! Elementary school is the first step toward becoming a teenager. What happens there effects what happens in middle school, which effects what happens in high school, which effects what happens for the rest of your life!

After middle school, I was assigned to go to one of two schools for high school. My options were the really small, very overpopulated school or the school where each of my worst bullies would be in every class. I was certain that, these being my only two choices, I would just kill myself. Luckily, my mother, saint that she is, found a private school for me and brought me there instead. It was a fresh new start. No one knew I couldn't read a hand clock. No one knew I had anger management issues that were brought on by stress. A clean slate, so to speak.

But middle school had me completely unprepared for high school. It left me shy and introverted. Fortunately, though, when I got to high school, Mr. Fry changed all that. The Fry Guy, as I called him, always paid attention to me as a person. Where most teachers saw me as a name with a check next to it on the absentee list, he saw me as Steven How-Weird—the fifteen-year-old guy who had two sisters and a dog named Fritz, who could draw and write really well, and who loved Power Rangers. He was everything a teacher should be—happy, welcoming, and helpful. He helped me through the roughest times at that school. When my girlfriend broke up with me, he was there. He even went so far as to hug me when I cried at the end of that story.

So, that's my story. I know it's just one of literally billions of teenage stories. I suppose you're wondering how to relate to, or understand, teens better. Having worked with teens, I have some experience; but especially because I was one, I remember what it was like.

And you were once one too! People tend to forget that in the past they were teens themselves. It's easy to tell someone what they should have done or what you would do if you were in their shoes. It's harder to remember that the life experiences adults have faced change a person in ways that a teenager hasn't yet been affected by, because they haven't yet experienced those things. It's like telling a baby to run when they can't even crawl yet.

The best way to help the teens in your life is to look at them as a person and expect that person to behave slightly less mature than you. Always give the benefit of the doubt when judging a person's character. During your experiences with this person, you can also lower or heighten your expectations of him, depending on what he does. For example, if he makes twelve mistakes on his homework that you clearly would not have made, you can lower your expectation of his ability to learn that subject.

The next step in relating to a teenager is to help change the person so that he is equal to or surpasses you in the areas where he needs help. Keep in mind that some people like to wait until they are comfortable before they move up the staircase. Be patient—they will get there. As a teacher, it is your job to challenge him to get even better in the areas where the person excels.

There is no such thing as best; people can always get better. As a parent, it's crucial to use what you already know about your teenager to affect how you judge him on how well he does. The goal should be that the teenager will become a person who you are not only proud of but someone you might even aspire to be.

The Infinite Us

B. Michael Hall
Age 17
Rockville, Maryland

The long shadows of the trees reminded us how far we were from the "beaten path." From the literal path we were perhaps fifty feet, but from what was so often regarded as the symbolic path, we had strayed perhaps a bit farther. There were six of us striding over the understory of the local suburban attempt at a deciduous forest. The façade was almost believable, save that all of the trees were within a yard of being the same height. There was no foliage around us, just bare trunks of aspen. The autumn trees were bare, and the shadows of their fingers seemed to reach around us as we crunched through the dull fallen leaves.

Although the moon's light was dim, a house up ahead was lit by surrounding floodlights, creating shadows that were not only twisted but stark and unnatural. We drew near our destination and felt a stirring somewhere between our hearts and stomachs. It was a two-story house with plywood over the doors and first-floor windows. Wide patches of outside wall stood out, weathered by time and neglect, the white paint worn down and the siding torn and punctured. A large stamp that read "NO TRESPASSING" in an authoritative black sans serif font stretched across the front of the house.

Each of us had our own independent reaction to the sign. George ignored it, or rather, tried to deny its presence by refusing to acknowledge it; Sanjit swore at it; Avinash looked at Collin for guidance; Arya flinched as though the letters leaped off and struck him; Collin shrugged and looked around for cops—of course there were none; and Daniel scanned for cops as well, seeing them in the shadows of the trees where no policemen actually lurked. Arya and Daniel met eyes and, each knowing then that they were not alone, said, "We'll stay here."

George asked, "The fuck for?" Profanity was for George an avocation, not an occasion.

Arya nearly backed down, but Daniel took up their cause. "We're not getting caught doing this stupid shit. Tell us how it goes."

"Don't be a pussy," said George. "This is why we're here, it's not like I wanna be awake right now. It's to do stuff like this…it's for the *adventure*, man. Can't have fun without some risk."

"Come on," contributed Collin, "it's not like the floodlight guy called the cops."

"Let them be," said Sanjit coolly. "It's their choice."

George always deferred to Sanjit, though none of us knew why, as he was firmly against authority and tonight was no exception. He shrugged—his hands up by his shoulders palms-forward. *I'll back off* was the message. Collin nodded.

Arya laughed, trying to play it off, knowing he'd lost face. "Besides," he joked, "it's probably a serial killer in there, and I'll pass."

"Probably a hobo," said George, who couldn't bear to let another have the last word.

I was, in fact, one of the aforementioned six, but as the night progressed, I became a piece of all of them. Somewhere amidst the tangled shadows the lines between us became as lost as those between the ghosts of the forest brought out by the harsh white floodlights. The risk we were taking, the idiocy of the whole endeavor of exploring the neighborhood at two in the morning, the quiet of the woods edging us together allowed us to all mingle together as parts of *US.* And while Daniel and Arya elected not to approach the house, I continued, yet I also felt their apprehension, their fear. It was not cowardice; it was merely that cold-footed feeling that afflicts the adolescent when he feels unable to hide among the group.

As we continued, we all felt it in our stomachs as well—a nervousness that the boldest among us might have identified as fear, but which was not debilitating. What we felt instead was an exhilarating nervousness, one which made us aware of each nerve ending in our bodies and every aspect of the forest around us. We were more awake than we had ever been—to the feel of the cool autumn breeze, to the sound of leaves beneath our feet and of insects and animals singing in the night, to the texture of the knotty scarred tree trunks and the eroding pale house, to the scents of leaf and soil and clean air.

This nervousness carried us to the door of the house, which was closed against us and the other night-prowling kids of the neighborhood—who existed only hypothetically, but undoubtedly were out there somewhere. The door was whitewashed hardwood, grey-toned, with a rusted, well-worn brass handle—uninviting, unmoving, uncaring. Neutral to the risk we had taken in reaching it, unfeeling towards the contrasting thrill and relaxation we felt. "Should we kick it down?" George asked.

Sanjit, George, and Collin approached the door. Sanjit said, "We can't all kick it…the doorstep's not three people across."

Collin quickly, defensively, said, "I work out. I'm staying."

George was known to be the strongest of us; he folded his arms complacently.

Sanjit, quite possibly the best-natured among us, stepped down from the doorstep.

We braced ourselves for the kick, and our combined energy moved through Collin and George, into the door. However, neither Collin's thick boots and strong legs nor George's tennis shoes and angry kicks could budge it. We kicked again. We tried to concentrate our force on one spot. We switched Collin with Sanjit. We concentrated our blow again. Finally, we fit Sanjit, George, and Collin onto the step. Nothing could break the doorframe's embrace on the door.

"Maybe it's boarded up from the inside," Collin posited.

"Yeah," said George. "Let's find another way in."

We began to circle the house. Collin got his foot caught in a rabbit hole. "Meant to do that," he said before any of us could comment.

"Yeah, this shit'll kill you," George said a bit too loudly, intentionally projecting in the direction of Daniel and Arya.

Soon we came across a ladder. "*Balls* no," said Sanjit, who was a bit large; it was a very thin ladder. Sanjit was tall, dark-skinned, and wide-set, with round glasses and a few days' growth of beard, which along with scraggly black hair helped frame his aquiline face.

"I'm down," George responded.

"You're tiny," Sanjit fired back. True, George was short and lean—though his frame only hinted at his true strength—with buzz-cut sandy hair and an impish face, always laughing but never smiling.

Collin added, "Let's keep looking. We can come back." Collin was tall, lean, blonde, and absolutely, although wrongly, convinced that the urban look flattered his ivy-league looks.

We moved on around, coming to a bathroom window over what was apparently a basement. In the monochromatic floodlight, the white toilet was the same color as the rest of the room. For some time, we tried to kick in and pry out the bars, but to no avail.

Next we reached the back door; it was boarded up, as were the windows. By now the risk was less important to us than was the determination to make our forty-minute walk worthwhile.

Avinash, determined this time to initiate something, said, "I've got this, guys," and kicked the board. His kick, unlike ours earlier, did not belong to the group. He swore as a pain shot through his leg, and the door stayed shut.

We moved him aside and kicked it ourselves. On our second kick, he rejoined us. None of us could break the board.

Someone said, "Back to the ladder?"

And off we all went.

It took the strongest torsos among us, belonging to Sanjit and Collin, to lift the ladder—George's strength was in his arms and legs. Then we decided who would climb.

"I still can't," said Sanjit.

"I can," Avinash said. Avinash was not much thinner than Sanjit, and on the whole resembled him, save that he was a bit shorter and had a more angular face.

"No, you can't," George said.

Collin didn't want to contradict George, so he sacrificed Avinash's self-esteem for being appreciated. "I can," he stated, simply.

"So can Dan," George said as he realized it. "Say, Dan, wanna come over here?"

Torn, Dan blinked. But Arya gave him a significant look and he decided. "No!"

We turned away. "George," Collin declared, "you go first, we'll make sure it's safe and start with the smallest person first."

George nodded. Sanjit volunteered to hold the ladder under us. The ladder was at about a thirty degree angle from the house.

We went up one-by-one, slowly and carefully to mimic self-assurance, but truly to conceal our nervousness—for now we were wide awake, so aware that we felt every sway of the ladder, every gust of wind, every insecurity in the wood beneath us. As our awareness expanded, we expanded as well, and by the time we had reached the top of the ladder, looking down we had ascended Olympus—we were infinite, extending down the creaky ladder, across the forest that had carried us here, and extending up the ladder, into the mysteries of our final goal.

We walked through the upper rooms of the house; they were empty. The floor was covered in dust, save for the footprints of the now-confirmed hypothesis of predecessors. A few boards were missing, there were some holes in the walls, but overall, the second story was uninteresting. We next approached the stairs to find a ground-level entrance and let the rest of us in.

The entrance to the top of the staircase was boarded up. Two kicks yielded nothing, and we quickly saw another way, so we let it be.

The drywall over the staircase was visible and had worn away in several spots. George said, "Can you get down there if I kick it out?"

"If we kick it out—easy, yeah," Collin replied, changing the "I" to "we" for the sake of inclusion.

We kicked the drywall out, and Collin lowered himself onto the staircase. George followed. At the bottom of the stairs, impeding further advance, there was a massive pile of wooden boards, plastic shelves, a washer, and a lot of broken glass. Collin said, "I'll climb it first, I'm good at this kind of thing. Follow where I go."

George nodded, and we continued on our way, testing every step with a foot before committing. The mound shifted and collapsed in spots, but we navigated it, and included it in our all-encompassing expansion.

The floor was barren except for shards of broken glass and splinters of wood. We found that the front door was locked and bolted from the inside, with a heavy plank across it that was also bolted down. The house as a whole was eerily quiet, as though all of the little noises that the inhabitants had come to know in the house existed solely for its denizens, having vanished when the house was vacated—the inhabitants' ghosts, not those of the house itself.

We then tried the back door, because we remembered that the boards over it were on the outside of the house, and we thought we could kick them out from inside more easily. We got into place on either side of the board.

"One," George began the counting, the age-old count with its interminable meaning.

"Two," Collin continued.

"Three!" We cried out as we rushed for the door and kicked out as fiercely as we could; a month's worth of stress drawn out by the night's risks and the intimacy of its conversations came to a head in the soles of our shoes.

With a loud snap, the door gave way, and we realized it would have yielded to our slightest tap. As our touch had not been light, our feet carried on through the still air. Collin's leg overextended and he hurt the back of his knee; George knew enough to keep his knee bent but had so much momentum going that he stumbled through the sudden doorway and tripped on the board as it hit the ground. We recovered, all of our pent-up stress gone.

Our ascension was complete; an apotheosis, truly. We were deific—mortal law could not stop us, doors and signs and boards could not hinder us, we owned the night as Poseidon owned the sea, and what deities feel stress? What could God have to worry about? Our cares were vanquished with the board.

We brought ourselves back together as we met in the doorway; Collin and George transferred their experience to Sanjit and Avinash, and we continued our exploration. Avinash came across a broken jar labeled, "COPPER II ACETATE," and professed his discovery as though it were the Dead Sea Scrolls. Together we entered the basement, finding it wholly empty. It occurred to us to ask why the remaining items seemed to have all been piled in the center of the house, but no one was around to answer. Each of our theories was wilder than the last; I believe that our final opinion was that it was indeed the work of a serial killer, who lured people into his house to bore them to death. If so, we wondered inwardly whether our being fascinated meant that he had failed.

The basement having been fruitless, we next tried the garage, in which we found an empty bottle of holy water and a tin bottle of paint thinner, a few more splinters and shards notwithstanding. We decided then that it was time to go. We had conquered the foreboding house; it had been reduced to a story for our friends some other day, a proof of our ascension and of our belonging to the infinite *US*, of our *belonging*. I, for one, told this story at least ten times the next week, and certainly have told it thirty times since.

As we headed out, George picked up the paint thinner. "Can't sniffing this stuff get you high?"

"I think so," Collin answered, "but inhalants'll fuck you up, so I wouldn't do it."

George kept the bottle, and we left. We brought our full

group back together, and immediately the posturing began. The experience had been incredible, surely, but we could not yet quantify why. We had yet to understand that in that house we had developed a connection, with each other and with that house, that neighborhood, that forest, that story, a bond which the other two felt but did not possess. So, unable to reconcile the adolescent feelings with our juvenile minds, we instead glorified the literal experience, telling the story in turns, increasing our intensity until it reached an orgasmic level of recounting.

And, on through the dark forest we walked, away from the floodlights and the path, back towards the now-unnecessary safety of our neighborhood. Nonchalantly, George unscrewed the top of the bottle of paint thinner as we navigated the black forest using our phones as lanterns. He took a sniff. “I feel fine.” He then took a deep whiff.

“Dammit, George,” said Daniel. “Lay off it.”

“It’s no big deal,” George said, combatively. He walked over to Daniel and began to pour paint thinner on the ground in front of him while holding the bottle in front of his nose. Daniel jumped backwards, swearing loudly. Sanjit shushed him, as we were now drawing near a residential area and would not want to be heard or be too loud. Then he saw what George had done—“What the *fuck*, George? What the absolute fuck?”

George ran over to Sanjit and poured some out in front of him as well, then Collin, Avinash, and finally, the contents ran out on his way to Arya. He still gave no explanation. He then took a deep sniff of the empty bottle, then two, then three. Then, as though the high had been a prerequisite, he said, “Why the absolute fuck not?”

Within five minutes we could feel a dizziness in our heads, as though the very outside of our heads were spinning back and forth, leaving the centers as they were. Sanjit and Collin developed coughs—when we complained to George about them, Avinash burst out coughing as well.

Within ten minutes, our throats were raspy, not quite like a sore throat, but rather, sore in our windpipes; our breaths were ragged and brought more coughing. At the same time, the world was tilting left and right around us, revolving no longer about the poles to the north and south but about *us,* we were central in our high and in our ecstasy over what we had done; for a brief moment, the sum of the world was found between us six.

We arrived at Sanjit's house, from which we had embarked. The high had worn off; what our newfound infinity needed now was confirmation, an audience. We received ours at school the next day.

In the morning, before the bell rang for class, we grouped together and reminisced on the night's events as Vietnam veterans are said to do about the war, as thieves do over their last big score. We did so loudly enough that those around us could hear, and our usual associations were enthralled.

We transcended the question of who went how far into the house. As the story was told in its evolution, Daniel and Arya were brave and willing lookouts, George and Collin bold pioneers, Sanjit and Avinash patient strongmen carrying the ladder for their friends.

Such is adolescence, a time in which nervous kids embark together, each determined to conform, discovering through their journey that to conform is not the goal, but instead, to come together, to discover that out of individual disparity the collective strength increases, that each has his or her own place to fill as the world rotates uncaringly around us, as we ascend our own infinity. Such is being a teenager, discovering that room to explore is more important than any lesson given by another, be it adult or teenager or child.

Recommended Reading

Ainslie, Tom, and Bonnie Ledbetter. *The Body Language of Horses.* New York: William Morrow and Company, Inc, 1980.

Camp, Joe. *The Soul of a Horse*. New York: Harmony Books, 2008.

Grandin, Temple. "Horses," in *Animals Make Us Human.* (Orlando: Houghton Mifflin Harcourt Publishing Company, 2009) 105-35.

Hill, Cherry. *How To Think Like A Horse.* North Adams: Storey Publishing, 2006.

Irwin, Chris. *Horses Don't Lie.* New York: Marlowe & Company, 2001.

Rashid, Mark. *Life Lessons from a Ranch Horse.* Boulder: Johnson Books, 2003.

Roberts, Monty. *The Man Who Listens To Horses.* London: Random House, 1996.

Webb, Wyatt. *It's Not About the Horse.* Carlsbad: Hay House, 2002.

Tools for Enticing Teens to Talk

Esteem Archi Tecture created by Jill Campbell and Barry Kaufman
Phoenix Publishing International
800-345-0325

Teen Talk cards by Free Spirit Publishing
www.freespirit.com
800-735-7323

The Ungame – Teen Version by Talicor, Inc.
www.talicor.com
800-433-4263

Totika Principles, Values, Beliefs Cards
by Western Psychological Services
www.wpspublish.com

About the Author

Heather Kirby is a Licensed Clinical Social Worker, a Certified Substance Abuse Counselor, and holds a Master's degree in Special Education. She has spent over twenty years working directly with children, adolescents, and families in a variety of mental health and special education settings. Heather specializes in reaching difficult teens through alternative therapies and has created her own activity-based therapeutic approach called Facilitated Socialization™. She was one of the first graduates of Melisa Pearce's certification program in the Equine Gestalt Coaching Method™ and has completed the advanced training in Trauma-Focused Equine Assisted Psychotherapy with Tim and Bettina Jobes.

In 2011, Heather was recruited to develop an equine therapy program for Childhelp, a national organization providing residential treatment for children who are survivors of traumatic abuse and neglect. The position allowed her to combine her passion for equine therapy with her skills as a clinician and her talent for program development. Currently, Heather works in private practice, with offices in Bethesda, MD and Fairfax, VA, and provides equine therapy through a partnership with Project Horse, Inc. in Purcellville, VA.

Heather's unique background allows her to look through a variety of lenses and draw upon experience in the fields of substance abuse, education, recreation, and mental health. She is also a dynamic speaker and offers trainings and workshops on a variety of different topics, tailoring each to the individual needs of the target audience.

Heather resides in Springfield, VA with her fabulous partner, their wonderful dog, and an amazing little hamster. She can be reached by email, phone, Facebook, or through her website.

Heather@KCClinicalSolutions.com
703-409-2571
www.KCClinicalSolutions.com

About the Press

Merry Dissonance Press is a book producer/indie publisher of works of transformation, inspiration, exploration, and illumination. MDP takes a holistic approach to bringing books into the world that make a little noise and create dissonance within the whole in order that ALL can be resolved to produce beautiful harmonies.

Merry Dissonance Press works with its authors every step of the way to craft the finest books and help promote them. Dedicated to publishing award-winning books, we strive to support talented writers and assist them to discover, claim, and refine their own distinct voice. Merry Dissonance Press is the place where collaboration and facilitation of our shared human experiences join together to make a difference in our world.

Visit http://merrydissonancepress.com/ for more information.